SLIM BRU

(1903–1990)

I was in the clink in 1919 for being a Wobbly. I was run out of town in Red Bluff, California for being broke. I wore chains in El Paso and stripes in St Augustine for the same reason. I've been investigated by all the law from the ward-heeler to the FBI for running a forum where free speech is guaranteed to all.

Brother, I know what the police state is.

O

Let me give thanks that I have been a jailbird, Beatnik, hungry bum and underprivileged kid. Also, that I have worked with my hands most of my life. That's the way most of the world lives.

O

Being president emeritus of the Hobo College and Janitor of the College of Complexes, I can speak as one educator to another.

Learn to Complain without suffering

Bughouse Square Series

CHARLES H. KERR
Established 1886

Slim Brundage, Founder & Janitor

SLIM BRUNDAGE

From
BUGHOUSE SQUARE
to the
BEAT GENERATION

Selected Ravings

Edited & Introduced by
Franklin Rosemont

Bughouse Square Series

Chicago
CHARLES H. KERR PUBLISHING COMPANY
1997

On the Cover:
Photo-booth self-portrait snapshots
of Slim Brundage
(late 1920s)

The drawings on pages 51 and 135 are from
George L. Carlson's
1001 Riddles for Children (1949).

ISBN 0-88286-232-4 (paper)
First Edition

❀ Printed on recycled paper.

WANTED

For future publishing projects: Photographs, publications, art-
work, memorabilia, personal accounts, information and
ephemera concerning Bughouse Square and other free-speech
forums, hobo colleges, the Dil Pickle Club, the College of Complexes, the IWW, Chicago anarchism, and early (especially pre-
1900) Charles H. Kerr publications. Please contact the editor of
this volume c/o the Charles H. Kerr Publishing Company, 1740
West Greenleaf Avenue, Chicago IL 60626, or leave a message at
773-465-7774.

For a calendar of meetings of
The College of Complexes
call (312) 326-2120.

 594

Write for our catalog.
Charles H. Kerr Publishing Company
Established 1886
P. O. Box 914
Chicago, Illinois 60690

TABLE OF CONTENTS

II. Ravings: The Janitor of the College of Complexes Challenges the Military-Industrial Complex

ACKNOWLEDGEMENTS

My personal acquaintance with Slim Brundage started long after the period covered in the articles collected here, but I did get to know the illustrious Janitor in his later years *via* telephone and the combined services of the U.S. and Mexican post offices. It was Brundage's hope that the Charles H. Kerr Publishing Company, whose books helped him evolve from hobo and Wobbly to hobo and Wobbly scholar and educator, would one day bring out a book of his. It is good to see this dream realized at last.

In preparing this collection I have benefitted from conversations, correspondence and interviews with many of Slim Brundage's friends, associates and relatives, including William J. Adelman, Brad Carlson, Carlos Cortez, Leon Despres, Kenan Heise, Ella Jenkins, Leonard Karlin, Maynard Krasne, Jim and Elsie Mach, Burr McCloskey, Jack Micheline, Henry J. Oettinger, Joe Segal, Jack Sheridan (the younger), Ruth Sheridan, Joffre Stewart, Meta Toerber and Jenny Lahti Velsek.

Many of these friends also kindly shared their reminiscences of Bughouse Square, the Dil Pickle Club, the Industrial Workers of the World (IWW), the Charles H. Kerr Publishing Company, the Radical Bookshop, Studio Players, the Proletarian Party, the Free Society Group, the Hobo Colleges, the early years of the College of Complexes, the Chicago jazz scene, and the farflung radical workingclass community and counterculture in which they all flourished. Others who offered valuable information along the same lines include Margaret Burroughs, Harry Busck, Carl Cowl, Ruth Dear, Al Glotzer, Robert Green, Pat Harbeck, James "Bozo" Kodl, Karl Meyer, Martin Ptacek, Ralph W. Rieder, Sally Kaye Rosemont (my mother), Sal Salerno, Steven Sapolsky, Harry Siitonen, William Targ, Studs Terkel and Geraldine Udell.

Many old friends and fellow workers who have long since passed away also provided important insights and details that I have drawn on in my Introduction, and I want to acknowledge them here: Gertrude Abercrombie, Irving Abrams, Nelson Algren, Carl Berreitter, Katherine Brundage, Sam Calender, Jack Conroy, Sam and Esther Dolgoff, St Clair Drake, Joseph S.

Giganti, Sarah Gruber, Joseph Jacobs, Meridel LeSueur, Katherine Kerr Moore (daughter of Charles H. Kerr), Joe Niver, Henry P. Rosemont (my father), Walter Schonbrun, Jack Sheridan, Fred Thompson, Virgil Vogel, Arthur Weinberg and Al Wysocki.

Charles Paidock, current program director of the College of Complexes, helped put me in touch with College old-timers.

My appreciation of the Dada movement and its influence, as discussed in Part IV of the Introduction, was appreciably deepened by an evening with Man Ray in Paris, 1966; by lengthy discussions with several of my fellow participants in the Surrealist Group at the time, especially the late Robert Benayoun and Jean-Claude Silbermann, whose knowledge of the subject drew on their own association with such notable ex-Dadas as André Breton and Benjamin Péret; and by many discussions with my good friend E. F. Granell, who also happens to have been a good friend of Marcel Duchamp.

The rise and fall of the Beat Generation, and its multifarious ramifications in Chicago and elsewhere (touched on in Part VI of the Introduction), are topics I have discussed over the years with many friends, including the late Eddie Balchowski, Paul Buhle, Carlos Cortez, the late Robert Fitzgerald, Paul Garon, Morgan Gibson, Robert Green, Joseph Jablonski, Ted Joans, Natalie Kenvin, Philip Lamantia, Warren Leming, Tristan Meinecke, Jack Micheline, Harvey Plotnick, Charles Radcliffe, Dave Roediger, June Skinner Sawyers, Harry Siitonen, the late Bruce E. Sloan, Joffre Stewart and ruth weiss, and I am grateful to all of them for sharing their knowledge and ideas.

Thanks to Diana Haskell and the staff at Newberry Library for their assistance in going through the Newberry's collection of Dil Pickle Club materials, which helped clarify many details on the prehistory of the College of Complexes.

Special thanks to Carlos Cortez, Paul Garon, Archie Green, Lisa Oppenheim, Dave Roediger and Constance Rosemont for reading and commenting on the Introduction, and again to Constance Rosemont as well as to Justin O'Brien for invaluable technical assistance.

And thanks above all to Penelope, as always, for sharing the secret of Cold Mountain's many hidden wonders.

F.R.

This book is dedicated to my mother,
SALLY KAYE ROSEMONT,
Pioneer Jazzwoman & Radio Comedienne,
the Chicago Theater's "Boop-boop-a-doo Girl"
(1929–1930),
and President of Chicago's
Organized Women Musicians
(1965–66).

*"How long can you talk into a microphone
without saying something funny?"*

Pencil portrait of Slim Brundage by Margaret Brundage (*c.* 1932)

INTRODUCTION TO THE LIFE
AND RAVINGS OF SLIM BRUNDAGE

Apparently anything that makes life interesting
is dangerous to the existing order.
—Robert E. Park
(*The City*, 1925)

I. A COLLEGE UNLIKE ANY OTHER

FEW EDUCATIONAL institutions of the past fifty years have exemplified the notion of a *community of scholars* more than Chicago's College of Complexes.[1] American universities can boast of scholars galore, but the lack of community in these semifeudal, ultrahierarchical and hypercompetitive institutions, not to mention their notorious indifference to the larger communities around them, is nothing short of appalling. In the College of Complexes the relation of teacher and student (labels rarely used, by the way, in College discourse), and of both to the surrounding neighborhood and broader culture, were based from the start on cooperation, mutual aid, humor and the pleasure principle.

Strictly speaking, the College of Complexes was a saloon, but its roster of lecturers, its open discussions and wall-to-wall blackboards distinguished it from every other watering-hole, just as its carnival atmosphere and emphasis on what a young Karl Marx once called "merciless criticism of everything in existence"[2] made it impossible to confuse it with any ordinary center of learning.

A kind of modern-urban-nightclub version of Brook Farm, the College billed itself as The Playground for People Who Think—a place where learning and having fun were not regarded as irreconcilable opposites. Indeed, during the heyday of the College from around 1955 through 1960, humor, pleasure and kicks were held to be not only as important as education, but also as essential components of it.

At the College, moreover, "No subject was sacrosanct, no theme was taboo."[3] Openness was the basic ingredient of its creative talkfests. Each and every person could speak, restricted only by a pre-agreed-on time-limit. Participants in these intellectual free-for-alls found them invigorating, and even those who came just to look and listen—or even to scoff—usually went home feeling "high" as well as wiser and better-informed.

Looking through old issues of the College's monthly house-organ, *The Curriculum*, one is first impressed by the incredible range of matters under discussion there, and the hilarious balance between the deadly serious and the seemingly frivolous. Debate topics included: "Was Karl Marx a Schnook or a Good Guy?" "Did the U.S. Lose World War II?" "Will Sex Ever Displace Baseball as a National Pastime?" and "Are Beatniks Useless?" Scholarly lectures on philosophers (Plato, Kierkegaard, Nietzsche, Sartre and many others), psychoanalysis, juvenile delinquency, Louis the XIVth, Edward Bellamy, Karl Marx, Lesbianism, the Taft-Hartley Act, Mahatma Gandhi, women's reproductive rights, the French Revolution, Ammon Hennacy, pornography, Relativity Theory and the *Bhagavad-Gita* were interspersed with demonstrations of hypnosis, ventriloquism, handwriting analysis and fencing. Group discussions took up such questions as: "Why Do All World War II Novels Stink?"[4] "Why Is America Defending Colonialism?" "Should Marijuana Laws Be Repealed?" and "Why the Next President Should Be Shot Into Space."

Many meetings (rarely called "classes," no doubt because the College upheld the ideal of a classless society) were devoted to Literature, several under the direction of radical novelist Jack Conroy, the Sage of Moberly, Missouri, and author of *The Disinherited* (1933). The College's literary orientation, increasingly Beat in the years 1958–1960, was broad enough to include an evening in homage to A. E. Housman, a debate on Mark Twain (on his 117th birthday), and Elsie MacMahon's lectures on the work of the Marquis de Sade.

The College, moreover, was *the* place for poetry-readings in Chicago during the late 1950s. Those who read more than once included local Beats Kent Foreman and Joffre Stewart, near-Beat Ken Nordine (who presented several sessions of "Word Jazz"), and on-the-road Beat Jack Micheline, as well as such colorful non-Beats as Bert Weber, poet laureate of the legendary hobohemian Dil Pickle Club[5] of the 1920s, and former

12

Ziegfield Follies star Frances Stuart Kenyon, who read to her own piano accompaniment.

The Fine Arts were not neglected. Many local painters, photographers and sculptors, including Erin Libby, Jac Worth, Ray Olson, Art Sheldon, Max Marek and John Krtzon (better known as John the Garbage Man), exhibited work at the College. Few of them made waves in the Art Market, but they were College "characters," one and all. As a "playground," the College took a special interest in participatory art. *The Curriculum* reports comedian Jerry Colonna supervising a moustache-drawing contest, a prize offered for the best painting of a "complex," and "Doodle Night," during which the perpetrator of the best doodle received five dollars credit.

A wide variety of music was played there: folk, jazz, blues, ethnic, classical and tin-pan-alley. Big Bill Broonzy often played at the Wednesday evening Folk Nights; Ella Jenkins was a College "regular" for years. Where else but the College could you listen to live music played on the Japanese samisen, Hungarian cymbaline, Scottish bagpipes and Russian balalaika—all in one night? Many evenings were given to the art of dance: African, Afro-Cuban, Latin American, modern, social, jazz and even square.

Students of cinema could savor the subtleties of Charlie Chaplin, W. C. Fields and Laurel and Hardy shorts at College Film Nights, along with an occasional documentary. Sometimes the weekly "Book Review" considered a film instead.

"Aside from the South Side jazz clubs," recalls College habitué Maynard Krasne, "in those years there were only two places to go in Chicago for first-class entertainment: the Clark Theater and the College of Complexes." At the College, there was "something doing" seven nights a week. But the heart of a good College of Complexes education lay in the group discussions of current events—political, social, economic, cultural and sexual questions. These were a constant, ongoing part of the College curriculum, and contributed, more than any other single factor, to the unique flavor of the place. As with the courses on history and poetry, the accent in these symposia, round-robins and debates was on the controversial, the unorthodox, the radical. Now and then Congressmen, businessmen, policemen and even unabashed right-wingers addressed the forum, but the great majority of College meetings assembled under the tutelage of Far Left malcontents: anarchists, Marxists, socialists, small-c communists, revolutionary pacifists, Wobblies, beatniks, and others who may have eschewed isms but felt at ease only in such anti-Establishment company.

All manner of unpopular and lost causes, especially those given short shrift in the media, were given top priority at the College. Hardly a week went by without major addresses by ban-the-bomb and antiwar militants, civil-rights activists, opponents of censorship and advocates of sexual freedom. Exposés of imperialism, police and other civic corruption, and the spineless ineptitude of the official U.S. labor movement, were always on the agenda. Burr McCloskey, who came to be known as "The Man Who Will Not Let Haymarket Die," spoke again and again on the judicial murder of the Chicago anarchists in 1887, and its meaning for today. The orientation of the College was as non-Stalinist as could be, but at the height of the 1950s McCarthyist Red Scare, Communist Party leader Claude Lightfoot and others were invited to defend the Party against the barrage of propaganda from the House Un-American Activities Committee.

Unlike the traditional Left, which tended to fetishize archaic programs and to approach anything new with utmost trepidation, the College always welcomed extremists, eccentrics, oddballs. Nudists, vegetarians, single-taxers and others widely regarded as "cranks" found a sympathetic platform at the College. It was one of the few places where the pressure to conform was in abeyance, where "being different" was an asset. Rebels with and without causes made it a home away from home.

Alongside its specifically educational and recreational functions, the College thus provided a rare living link between the subterranean hobo/Wobbly/Bughouse Square counterculture of the 1910s and '20s, and the post-Beat/New Left counterculture of the 1960s. Recognized by old-timers as the direct heir of the Dil Pickle, the College was also known—to police and public alike—as the city's foremost "beatnik bistro."

No wonder this "very interesting place"—as old-time Wobbly Jenny Velsek has described it—soon became a hangout for nonconformists of all kinds, and one of the "sights to see" for curiosity-seekers and tourists as well as visiting poets and scholars. Gwendolyn Brooks, Carl Sandburg, Nelson Algren, Duke Ellington, Roger Baldwin (founder of the American Civil Liberties Union), Studs Terkel, Willard Motley, Albert Goldman (Leon Trotsky's lawyer), Congressman Sidney Yates, Elmer Gertz, Leon Despres, A.J. Muste, Tony Bennett and Sid Lens are only a few of those who made the scene at the College. For several years running it was surely the best show in town. Compared to the College, as its alumni have often pointed out, the Oprah and Geraldo TV shows are pitiably namby-pamby versions of what truly free discussion can be.

II. How One Becomes a Janitor

Slim Brundage (1903-1990) was the founder and guiding genius of this unique citadel of laughter and learning. Hobo, Wobbly, jailbird, Bughouse Square and Bug Club soapboxer, Dil Pickler, president emeritus of the old Hobo College, housepainter, humorist and permanent public nuisance, he was certainly the right man for the job.

Born in 1903 in the Blackfoot, Idaho lunatic asylum, where both his parents worked, Myron Reed Brundage always despised his first and middle names and insisted on being addressed as Slim—the archetypal hobo moniker. Similarly, in later years, although his counterparts at more formal educational establishments bore such titles as Chancellor or Rector, Brundage—with characteristic hobo pride, often mistaken for modesty—preferred to be known simply as the College janitor. This was no empty "honorary" title; few visitors to the College missed seeing Brundage in his janitorial raiment, mop in hand, cleaning the College floors.

He was raised by his father, a jack-of-all-trades socialist and sometimes newspaperman, but it was as a hobo that Brundage's real education began. The grade-school dropout who had learned next to nothing in school (from twenty-four teachers in seven and a half years) took to the road at fourteen and learned fast and plenty from fellow 'boes in the jungles, in freight cars, and in many a small-town jail where he and his colleagues were often confined as "vagrants." Grad school began at sixteen when he took out a Red Card in the Industrial Workers of the World (IWW), or Wobblies, in Aberdeen, Washington, and became a delegate (organizer) a week later. A revolutionary industrial union founded only a few years earlier (in Chicago, 1905), the IWW pioneered in the organization of unskilled, foreign-born and migratory workers, who were then shunned as "unorganizable" by the American Federation of Labor (AFL). Thanks to the bold, imaginative spirit and daring, innovative tactics manifest in their epochmaking strikes and free-speech fights, the Wobblies' legacy remains the brightest of all in the annals of U.S. labor. As a Wobbly, Brundage's personal experiences of political/economic reality in the U.S.A. acquired a deeper meaning for him as he regarded it anew from the solid grounding of revolutionary theory. The things he learned from IWW literature and the Charles H. Kerr Company's "Library of Socialist Classics" stayed with him for life. His fellow Wobs' deep appreciation of poetry, philosophy, history and the natural world also heightened his sense of the good things in life, and helped him develop a sound morality based on workingclass self-emancipation and international solidarity.

Brundage landed in Chicago in 1922 and, apart from a few infrequent trips, made his home there until he retired to Mexico in 1975. Within days of his arrival in the city he resumed his studies. Postgraduate courses in what he called "subversive forensic" at Chicago's open forums—the South Side outdoor Bug Club, the Near North Side Bughouse Square, and the nearby indoor Dil Pickle Club at 18 Tooker Alley—sharpened his ability to think for himself, and especially to think on his feet, to articulate his thoughts quickly and effectively, with inspiration and humor. To successfully fend off hostile hecklers without alienating a large crowd can be a delicate task, requiring great skill and large quantities of wit. Wobblies were past masters of the art; indeed, the One Big Union was the greatest school of stand-up comics this country has ever seen.

A housepainter by trade, Brundage was also active in the AFL Painters' Union, which he joined in Chicago in 1925. One of the largest of the building trades unions, the Painters had many locals in Chicago, with a combined membership in the thousands. Its members included many radicals: socialists, anarchists, Communists, Wobs and former Wobs. Communist Party co-founder Arne Swabeck, who later became a leading Trotsky-ist, and Dil Pickle manager Jack Jones are only two of the many well-known Chicago union painters who had once carried red cards in their pockets. Brundage was a member of Painters' Local 147 for many years, but later, in the 1940s, transferred to 637, one of the more democratic Scandinavian locals.

Although he waged some notable struggles in the union of his craft, he clearly felt more at ease in the classwide, multiracial, free-wheeling, openly revolutionary milieu of the IWW and the open forums. He was an assiduous frequenter of forums all over town throughout the 1920s and early '30s, and for several years starting in 1924 he worked at the Dil Pickle. When his friendship with Jack Jones turned sour, he began to dream of establishing a place of his own.

Brundage made an initial attempt to found a College of Complexes in 1933 but, notwithstanding a capital investment of forty dollars, it lasted only three months. In 1936, however, he became, at the age of thirty-three, director of the city's revived Hobo College, called The Knowledge Box. The future founder of this nation's most unique and nonconforming academy had no lack of credentials as an educator.

To his alma mater, the One Big Industrial Union, he often returned for refresher courses. Although he was not active in the IWW in later years, Brundage's respect for the union and its ideas, as well as for certain individual Wobs—most notably Fred Thompson, himself a distinguished educator[6]—was boundless. In *The Curriculum* for August 1956, which included a tribute to Thompson, Brundage described the IWW as "the most radical organization in America." His not-infrequent skirmishes with bureaucrats in the Chicago Painters' Union were inspired by IWW notions of rank-and-file control; the Council for Union Democracy, which he co-founded in 1943, was the forerunner and model of dozens of later and better-known intra-union reform groups.[7]

Socially, politically and culturally, his basic world-view remained IWW to the end. It would be impossible to exaggerate the overriding impact of the "Wobbly Experience"—that is, the combined and interacting experiences of hoboing, agitating, and participating in the IWW culture and its open-forum offshoots—on Slim Brundage. These are the complex forces that shaped the complex man who shaped the College of Complexes.

III. A COUNTERCULTURE THAT WON'T GO AWAY

Like most Wobblies, Brundage was an "avowed Marxist" who held that "the class struggle is the fundamental force in history."[8] To some, it may appear paradoxical—or a sign of intellectual incompetence—that he continued this statement by adding that he did "not believe in dialectical materialism." But the key word in this disclaimer, it seems to me, is *believe*. I suggest that Slim was not indicating his disagreement with Marxist methodology, but rather his non-acceptance of the conceit—too widely shared by would-be Marxists—that any mere *concept* could somehow, miraculously, contain the solutions to all problems. For the "areligious" Brundage, the truth of Marxism was not a matter of *faith*, but of deeds. Hoboes in general and Wobblies in particular learn to keep their eyes open; they tend to be much less interested in the application of doctrine than in drawing practical conclusions from life. Like many old Wobs, Slim in the 1950s and '60s saw that most of the new and vital energies in the struggle for a better world were emanating from sectors of the population that narrowminded Marxists had written off or belittled generations ago: kids, women, the so-called lumpenproletariat, Blacks, Native Americans, Chicanos, the handicapped, sexual nonconformists—not to mention such utterly unanticipated kinds of rebels as Hipsters and Beatniks.

Brundage's rejection of the "one-size-fits-all" models of Marxism thus turns out to be yet another proof of his hipness, as well as of his closeness to Marx's own way of thinking. His philosophical reflections may have lacked the veneer of sophistication, but his revolutionary proletarian reflexes were sharp and clear.

The College Janitor was, in effect, an exemplar of that mighty (if often underground) force in U.S. cultural history: the workingclass intellectual. Although such people are often called "self-taught" because they bypassed the more traditional and higher-priced centers of learning, they are truly products of a particular milieu that valued knowledge at least as highly as any cluster of Ph.D's in the halls of academe.

United by devotion to the cause of workingclass self-emancipation, a deep distrust of capitalist institutions, and a well-developed sense of proletarian democracy, this milieu once spanned the continent and beyond, and provided the backbone and moral fiber of the finest traditions of U.S. labor radicalism. In the Golden Age of the IWW and Gene Debs's Socialist Party, a class-conscious hobo could find kindred spirits in just about any city or town in the land. This nationwide vagabond *circuit*, not unlike the vaudeville circuit (with which, by the way, many 'boes were also connected), assured tramping scholars food to eat, food for thought and places to stay as well as places to soapbox and pass the hat.

In Chicago, America's hobo capital, this workingclass intellectual milieu seems to have proved stronger, more fruitful and more enduring than anywhere else in the country. In addition to the IWW, the Hobo College, the Dil Pickle Club and, later, the College of Complexes, its constituents included the anarchist Free Society Group, the group around the Charles H. Kerr Company, such small but vociferous Marxist groups as the Proletarian Party, the Communist League of America (Trotskyists), the Revolutionary Workers League ("Oehlerites"), the Communist League of Struggle ("Weisbordites"), the Libertarian Socialist League, and the "Council Communists."

It was a community served by numerous and generally short-lived newspapers, most with such titles as *Class Struggle* and *The Fighting Worker*, and by a long procession of "little magazines." In the 1930s, for example, there were E. J. Costello's weekly, *All Chicago* ("A Journal of Protest: Vital News or Views Not Found in Chicago Daily Newspapers"), an outgrowth of the Workers' Committee on Unemployment; and Joe Niver's *Earth* ("For Those Who Walk Abreast of the Whole Earth"), a Whitmanesque journal of poetry, fiction and ideas whose contributors included James T. Farrell, Ralph Chaplin, Jack Conroy, Ben Reitman, Parker Tyler and Jack Jones (several issues were printed on Jones' Dil Pickle Press).

Naturally, in a milieu that produced large quantities of such publications, bookstores played an important role. The Radical Bookshop on North Clark Street in the 1910s and '20s, Maury's in the late 1950s, and Solidarity Bookshop in the 1960s were not only purveyors of literature unavailable in other stores, but also places to meet and talk.

Chicago's "little theaters"—such as the Radical Bookshop's Studio Players (in which Brundage sometimes performed)—figured as part of this community, which also interacted at many levels with the local jazz and folk-music scenes. Other meeting-places included Bughouse Square, the Bug Club, dozens of other forums and—more informally, on Sunday mornings—the open-air market on Maxwell Street.

Thanks to Lucy Parsons and a few others, this dissident workingclass intellectual community, in which Slim Brundage made his debut in 1922, extended in an unbroken line back to pre-Haymarket days. From the moment it opened in January 1951, the College of Complexes became the most visible and accessible doorway to this pioneering counterculture.

The interconnections and cross-fertilizations between all these distinct component groups was extraordinary. The Charles H. Kerr Company supported the IWW from the beginning (many old-time radicals called it "that Wobbly publishing house") and numerous Wobs—Joe Hill, Ralph Chaplin, Vincent St. John, Elizabeth Gurley Flynn, Big Bill Haywood and many others—were closely associated with the Kerr Company and contributed to its *International Socialist Review*. Charles H. Kerr himself helped his friends, the Udells, set up the Radical Bookshop in the old Turner Hall building (in which the Haymarket anarchists used to meet in the 1880s), and the Kerr Company also had a big hand in starting the Dil Pickle Club. A half-century later, when the Chicago Branch of the IWW started Solidarity Bookshop, the Kerr Company—then run by Al Wysocki and a handful of other members of the Proletarian Party—provided a large selection of books on consignment.

Jack Jones, who early on became the Pickle proprietor, had left the IWW (with William Z. Foster) in a small but nasty 1912 split, and went on to concoct his own weird brand of techno-cratic politics which—to put it mildly—differed sharply from the views of his former fellow workers. Nonetheless, many Wobblies—including *Industrial Worker* editor Ralph Chaplin, poet Kenneth Rexroth and soapboxer Jack Sheridan—were active in Pickle affairs. A memorial for Chaplin organized "by some of the old Dil Picklers" took place at the College of Complexes in 1960. Sheridan took part in College activities for years.

Fred Thompson was no Dil Pickler, but he and Sheridan—and countless other Wobs—were frequent speakers at Bughouse Square. A radical since his teens in Canada in the 1910s, when his comrades included an elderly English Chartist and veterans of the Knights of Labor, Thompson became the best-known Wobbly of the 1950s and '60s. More than any other individual, he served as liaison between old-timers and younger Wobs such as Dick Ellington, Utah Phillips and the surrealist-oriented group known as "the left-wing of the Beat Generation" who ran Solidarity Bookshop.

The Free Society Group was one of the largest and most active anarchist groups in the country from the 1920s through the 1950s. Among its members were some of the best-known figures in twentieth-century anarchism: Russian anarcho-syndicalist Gregori Maximoff, best-remembered for his translations of Bakunin; Boris Yelensky, also Russian, and a friend of Kropotkin's; Spanish-born Maximiliano Olay, veteran of great labor struggles in Cuba and among immigrants in Tampa, Florida, and the official U.S. representative of the Spanish Confederation of Labor (CNT) during the 1936 Revolution; and several Italians who had been close to Errico Malatesta in the old days. It was under Free Society auspices that Rudolf Rocker and Emma Goldman spoke on their visits to Chicago. From the late 1930s until it faded out in the early '60s the Free Society Group and its offshoot, the Alexander Berkman Aid Fund, used the IWW hall at 2422 North Halsted as its meetingplace and mailing-address. Several Free Society comrades, including Arthur Weinberg—later well-known as the biographer of Clarence Darrow—were also active in the IWW, and the two groups often arranged joint picnics. Weinberg also spoke at the College.

Despite political and cultural divergences, this milieu was held together by extensive informal associations that were often strengthened by close personal ties. In the thick of it all, decade after decade, Slim Brundage played a central and animating role. Consider this anecdote: At a 1971 *bon voyage* party for anarchist/Wobbly Carlos Cortez and his wife Marianna, who were leaving on a trip to Europe, Fred Thompson, longtime socialist

Virgil Vogel and others learned that Al Wysocki was ill and no longer able to carry on the day-to-day operations of the old Kerr Company. Their decision, right then and there, to do what they could to keep the Kerr Company going, soon led to a full-fledged revival of the publishing house, in which they were joined by yet another veteran Red, Joe Giganti. As a young Communist in the 1920s, Giganti had served as editor and opera-reviewer for the Party's Italian daily, and directed local Sacco-Vanzetti defense agitation; expelled as a "Trotskyite" in 1928, he was later active in the Oehlerite RWL and became a close friend of anarchist Maximiliano Olay. What is important, in the present context, is this: Vogel, Thompson, Giganti and Cortez all hailed from very different Left backgrounds and pursued individual activities that frequently had little in common with that of the others, but nonetheless thought of themselves as active participants in a coherent and recognizable radical community. Each at different times served as president of the Charles H. Kerr Company's Board of Directors (Cortez holds this position today). And every one of them was a friend of Slim Brundage's and active in the College of Complexes.

Symbolizing the Janitor's identification with this community of rebel workers, his ashes are interred near the Haymarket martyrs' monument at Waldheim (Forest Home) Cemetery in Forest Park—the final resting-place of the Haymarket anarchists, Voltairine de Cleyre, Joe Hill, Lucy Parsons, Nina Spies, Big Bill Haywood, Ben Reitman, Elizabeth Gurley Flynn, Fred Thompson and many other Wobblies, Dil Picklers and fighters of the good fight.

IV. CAN DADA SOLVE THE SCHOOL CRISIS?

The aim of the College of Complexes, as an educational/recreational forum, was neither to recruit members nor to mobilize troops for the achievement of specific goals, but rather to inform, agitate, educate, emancipate, provoke, inspire, offend, scandalize, tickle and excite. Its status as a non- or anti-organization, the range and unusualness of its activities, its emphasis on improvisation and "goofing off" all served to distinguish the College from everything else that was happening on what passed for the Left in those years. These very qualities also made it a precursor or testing-ground for such later manifestations of oppositional culture as Second City (in its early days), the "guerrilla theater" of the late Sixties, and the more recently developed radical fringe of "Performance Art."

The playful, open-ended, let's-see-what-happens radicalism that defined Brundage's—and the College's—overall praxis was largely a legacy from the IWW and the forums it spawned, but there was also a dash of Dada in it. I would go so far as to say that the secret of the College's remarkable appeal and staying-power lies precisely in its rare synthesis of these two inexhaustible inspirations.

Although historians have ignored it, Dada was a very real presence in Chicago from the first year of Prohibition (1920) to the last (1933). It didn't bother much with labels or credentials, but Windy City Dada was the real thing, fresh from Berlin and Paris, and those who took it up here were responding to the same moral and political exigencies as their European and Japanese co-conspirators across the seas.

Reporting on the German Revolution for the *Chicago Daily News*, Ben Hecht fell in with George Grosz and other Berlin Dadas and even took part in one of their largest exhibitions. The *Chicago Literary Times*, which he co-edited with Max Bodenheim in 1923-24, was intended to "to attack everything," and that's what it did, with gusto. That it was an uneven mishmash does not alter the fact that it was also, in its better moments, a lively and provocative rag. Another local Dada nucleus, known as *The Escalator*, centered around Kenneth Rexroth and Lawrence Lipton. More tuned in to the Paris wing of the movement, it was also more consciously radical.

Chicago Dada's major outposts—frequented by both factions—were the Radical Bookshop on North Clark Street, and the Dil Pickle Club a little further down, a hop-skip-and-jump from Bughouse Square. Of course these were also prime hangouts for the youthful Janitor-to-be of the College of Complexes. Thus we see how easy it was for Slim Brundage, whose fluency in foreign languages was non-existent, to learn the essence of Dada from Those Who Knew, and without even leaving the very places where he felt most at home.

Of course, the stuff that Dada was made of was lying

around all over the place, in Chicago as elsewhere, and anyone could pick it up and fabricate Dadas and quasi-Dadas of their own, even without knowing it. Whether Brundage really got a whiff of Tristan Tzara's manifestoes is hardly the point. What matters is that, one way or another, his Wobbly trust in revolutionary creativity and spontaneity was reinforced and enhanced by a playful but desperate sense of nonsense, a free-wheeling sense of wild humor in which a defiant anti-rationalism provided the key to a whole new way of looking and living.

To some this may seem more like a recipe for the loonier forms of comedy, but in fact it was at the core of Brundage's radical theory of education. "There are *No Trespassing* signs on the minds of men as well as on real estate," he argued,[9] and his aim was to tear down those signs and to encourage people to venture beyond the well-worn tracks of stereotyped small talk, common sense and what old-time cartoonists called the "Daily Blah." Convinced that "a free and open forum is the best environment for self-expression,"[10] he set up the College to stimulate the broadest and most passionate exchange of ideas on any and all subjects—and the more controversial the better.

Rejecting the regimentation and routine of ordinary schools, the College instead promoted audacity and imagination, urging all to speak freely in an atmosphere of complete equality and camaraderie. Those who took part in this experiment in proletarian democracy, or creative anarchy, seem to have found it exhilarating. "What Slim did so well," as his friend Burr McCloskey pointed out, "was to exhort [everyone] to be unmuffled, ungagged, and unsilenced. What he did was to make it fun to think, fun to play with ideas, fun to speak up and to hell with the censors!"[11] In reminiscences of the College, few words turn up more often than *fun*. "The discussions were serious," College regular Henry J. Oettinger points out, "and the language could get vitriolic, but it was always in good fun." Beat poet Jack Micheline recalls, "I read there twice, and passed the hat afterward. I was an unknown poet at the time, but there was a good crowd, and I had fun there." Another regular, Elsie Mach, emphasizes that "*Everybody* had fun there." Musician/vocalist Ella Jenkins agrees: "It was a fun place to play at, and a fun place to go to." In contrast to the seriousness-for-the-sake-of-seriousness that makes most schools so boring, the College always put a premium on having a good time. Brundage knew, however—and this was the College's marvelous secret—that there is no better way of having a good time, intellectually speaking, than by challenging the rules, conventions and prejudices of the existing order.

V. An Outpost of Humor, Play, Equality and Other Un-American Activities

Systematically questioning all ruling ideologies helps undermine the repressive values and institutions these ideologies are supposed to uphold. In part because of the College's accessibility as a street-level pub, but above all because of its root-and-branch egalitarianism, this subversive game—which in other circumstances might have remained merely a *risqué* amusement for a handful of intellectuals—reverberated throughout the city and beyond.

No matter how earnest College group discussions were, they remained a *play activity*, and newcomers—even shy ones—found it easy to join the fun. The whole inhibition-lifting procedure probably owed something to Freud. Brundage's library from the early College days (the bulk of which he left at his wife Katherine's house when he retired to Mexico in 1975) included several well-read volumes on psychoanalysis, by Freud and others. Katherine Brundage, in the course of her long involvement with the Adler-influenced Chicago Community Child Guidance Center, was closely acquainted with local Adlerians and Adlerian literature. That the College's theory and practice drew on the experience of Freud and his colleagues is thus not so far-fetched as might appear at first sight.

Closer to home, I wonder whether the Janitor ever ran into the profound and revolutionary philosopher of play, Neva Leona Boyd (1876–1963), a social worker who directed the Chicago Training School for Playground Workers at Abraham Lincoln Center in the 1910s. Her work, posthumously collected (see Bibliography), overflows with surrealist/anarchist implications. Opposed to the moralistic, stereotyped and otherwise authoritarian forms of play imposed in schools, Boyd urges uninhibited free play—spontaneous, imaginative, dynamic, unconventional, collective, noncompetitive, repression-releasing and above all *pleasurable* (physically, emotionally, and intellectually)—as the soundest method of social education. Viewing play as *the creation of imaginative situations*, "a sort of vacation from one's everyday self and the routine of everyday living," she argues that the resulting "psychological freedom creates a condition in which strain and conflict are dissolved and potentialities are released." Far more than a mere "escape from reality," play for her is the open door to "a free realm in which persons are stimulated to create quite new emotional experiences and quite different social relationships"—experiences and relationships unthinkable, for example, "in the rigidity of routine work." In her view, such "fulfillment of potentialities" transforms the individual and opens the way to "a new collective life."

Although there is nothing to indicate that Brundage knew Neva Boyd or her ideas, it is certainly remarkable that her radical approach to play coincides so fully with the first principles of the College of Complexes.

As a learning experience, The Playground for People Who Think proved especially appealing to working people and minorities who, in those days even more so than now, were made to feel uncomfortable in universities. Here, too, the College's Wobbly legacy loomed large, for the IWW, more than any other union during the first third of the twentieth century, lived up to the promises made at its founding convention that Blacks, women, the poor and foreign-born would always be welcome in the One Big Union. "An injury to one is an injury to all!" was their motto. In a society afflicted with a white-supremacist ideology and power structure, the open forums courageously fostered anti-racist resistance.[12] One of the very few non-segregated nightspots on Chicago's North Side in Prohibition years was the Dil Pickle, where Lucy Parsons was a revered speaker and the visitors included former heavyweight champion Jack Johnson, Bob Crenshaw of the IWW, and young Harry Haywood, a militant of the African Blood Brotherhood. At the College of Complexes the active role of minorities was proportionally much larger.

Indeed, the College practiced Affirmative Action long before the expression was coined. Its Black speakers covered the whole spectrum of African-American politics in the pre-Black-

Panther years, from neo-Garveyist "Back to Africa" National-ists to revolutionary anarchopacifist Joffre Stewart. College meetings were addressed by journalists Roi Ottley and Louis Lomax, Beat poet Kent Foreman, Democratic Party alderman Ralph Metcalfe, former Olympic star Jesse Owens (Republican), Communist Claude Lightfoot, prominent officials of the Urban League and the N.A.A.C.P., as well as political figures from Africa, most notably Eduardo Mondlane, who spoke there in 1956 (thirteen years later, as president of the Mozambique Lib-eration Front, Dr Mondlane was assassinated in Dar-es-Salaam by agents of Portuguese colonialism). The College also offered numerous concerts by Black musicians, and performances by Black dancers such as Jimmie Payne, Claire Taggart, and the Robert Wells calypso troupe. Joe Segal's Jazz Showcase found a temporary home at the College while its new location was being readied. Ella Jenkins recalls that "A lot of blues people played there," too. College affairs were regularly reported in the local African American press—the *Defender* as well as the Chicago edition of the *Pittsburgh Courier*.

Like many Wobblies, Brundage had strong pacifist inclina-tions; that the workers of two or more countries should kill each other at the behest of their respective masters seemed to him utterly and monstrously wrong. His opposition to the draft, capitalist wars, bomb-testing and all militarism was absolute. He sympathized with Gandhian *Satyagraha* and sup-ported Martin Luther King's nonviolent civil rights actions in the South and in Chicago. Interestingly, his correspondence also reveals his admiration for revolutionary Black Nationalist Robert F. Williams, advocate of Black armed self-defense, as set forth in his book, *Negroes With Guns*. "I think you are the most dynamic rebel in America today," Brundage wrote him in May 1960. I have found no reference in the Janitor's papers to the single most influential Black revolutionary in the U.S., Malcolm X, but this lacuna is probably attributable to the fact that Mal-colm's explicitly revolutionary period began only when he broke with the conservative and inhibiting Nation of Islam in 1963—two years after the original College was shut down.

Curiously, during this period when the College was in limbo, Brundage printed a calling-card for himself that read:

Slim X Brundage. To what extent this was a nod to the greatest X of all time is not clear, but the card added a few illuminating terms of self-description: x-convict, x-college president, x-husband, x-bootlegger, x-painter, x-bartender, x-janitor, x-lover and "almost x-tinct."

As this enumeration of x's suggests, Brundage's relations with women were not always the happiest. Neither of his two marriages could be summed up as an unqualified success. Characteristically, however, he readily acknowledged that, both times, he chose his marriage partners largely "for their brains," and his wives were indeed remarkable women. His first bride, Margaret Johnson, whom he married in the late 1920s, was an artist, best-known for her marvelous, lurid covers for *Weird Tales*, the magazine in which H. P. Lovecraft and Clark Ashton Smith published much of their finest work.[13] Katherine Wood (Kay to her friends), who married Brundage in 1940, was fluent in Latin and Greek, earned degrees in drama and law and was also active in the Chicago Repertory Theater. Extensive correspondence indicates that, after his separation from Katherine, he had a prolonged affair with Helen McCloy, a former Paris correspondent for the Hearst papers and *New York Times* art critic, best known as the author of more than two dozen popular mystery novels, some regarded as classics.

Although his personal life seems to have had no shortage of conflicts and contradictions regarding what Marxists of his generation still called "The Woman Question," Brundage's marital troubles do not appear to have affected the College. His father had been a woman-suffrage advocate, and the Janitor himself, in his own odd and not always consistent way, was a kind of feminist. In *The Curriculum* for October 1960 he trashed old platitudes supporting male supremacy and reaffirmed the radical principle of women's equality—even superiority. "All the evidence I have," he wrote, "says woman is successful whenever she deigns to compete with men," and he goes on to argue that women are smarter, stronger, better mechanics and better doctors. He concluded that "women are all right in their place"—that is, everywhere *except* in the kitchen (the Janitor liked to do his own cooking).

One is tempted to discern here the early and ineradicable

influence of such dynamic Chicago characters as Martha Biegler, who ran the ultra-radical Woman's Forum in Dil Pickle days, Lillian Udell of the Radical Bookshop and Studio Players, and Lucy Parsons, whom the Chicago police regarded as "more dangerous than a thousand rioters."

In any event, the College featured women speakers from the start, and their number multiplied over the years. Among the women who addressed meetings were anarchists, socialists, pacifists, beatniks, a "striptease artist," a "Star Lady Wrestler," "America's most controversial exponent of exotic dancing," a policeman's wife, authors, poets, retired vaudevilleans, journalists and a few who surely qualify as feminists. Although that label was rarely used in those years, several women spoke on specifically feminist issues: on gender discrimination, for example, and the right to abortion.

Despite its occasional embarrassing "beauty contests" and corny sexist grafitti on the walls, the College welcomed women—as thinkers, social critics, creative individuals, comrades, fellow workers, equals—in ways that most schools, not to mention bars, did not. For many, the College marked a turning-point in their lives. Says Elsie Mach: "I was a Northwestern University student in those days, but it was at the College of Complexes that I learned about new and radical ideas." Where else in Chicago, in the over-tranquilized Eisenhower years, could free-spirited, feisty, independent women speak up and be heard? Until the Women's Liberation Movement took the country by storm at the end of the Sixties, the College was, locally, the only public forum truly accessible to radically nonconformist women.

Indeed, in 1950s Chicago, no public gatherings of any kind, anywhere—with the sole exception of Maxwell Street on Sunday mornings—were more interracial, or more multicultural, or more open to women, than the College of Complexes. Dupes of the middle-class American Dream no doubt considered it a hovel for weirdos. But deserters from the American Nightmare of class, racial, and gender oppression found it a haven, or at least a place where you could be yourself without being persecuted for it. The College never pretended to be a free sample of paradise, but it did try to foster an egalitarian climate in which human beings—in odd moments, after work or on weekends—could try to behave like human beings.

VI. BEATNIK PARTY WINS BY A LANDSLIDE!

Brundage was proud of the fact that he was born in a madhouse, and it is no accident that the name of his illustrious academy was drawn from the lexicon of psychopathology. The College house-organ was subtitled its "Official Neurosis," and the Janitor signed his "Ravings" column "Manic Depressive." A College matchbook, *circa* 1952, welcomed "all schizophrenics, manic-depressives, paranaoiacs, dementia-praecox, compulsives, etc." College regulars and faculty—those who hung around and pinch-hit for announced speakers who failed to show up—were designated "Schizos" or "Schizoids." Each carried a "Schizo Certificate," a small round-cornered card co-signed by the Janitor and whoever happened to be the in-house "Psychiatrist" at the moment. The card certified that the bearer, having been found "fully and satisfactorily wanting in sanity," was enrolled in the "Loyal Disorder of Schizos."

Implicit in such usage is the sense that the minority regarded as "insane" in this society tends to be more aware of the fundamental irrationality of the existing order than the obliviously obedient majority who boast of being "sane." To what degree this deliberate subversion of psychiatry's diagnostic vocabulary into terms of defiant self-affirmation was inspired by Dada, gleaned from other sources,[14] or independently discovered by the College research staff, has not been determined. But this much is clear: Brundage's use of the pejorative "crazy" as a high compliment accorded perfectly with Beat Generation protocol, and with the more general post-Hipster trend among American teenagers—as exemplified, for example, by Harvey Kurtzman's *Mad*, which started in October 1952, nearly two years after the College.

That Brundage and other College stalwarts responded so fraternally to the youth rebellion that eventually achieved mass-media notoriety as the Beat Generation would seem to be entirely in the order of things. Wouldn't lifelong agitators be expected to welcome a new agitation, especially at the height of the 1950s Cold War?

As it happened, most radicals of Brundage's age, and many who were younger, saw nothing in the Beat ferment but petit-bourgeois self-indulgence, withdrawal and the worst sort of foolishness.[15] Of the Dil Pickle veterans, apart from the Janitor, only Lawrence Lipton—who had relocated in Venice, California—threw in his lot with the Beats; his *Holy Barbarians* (1959) was the first and remains in many ways one of the best accounts of the Beat Generation as a social movement. Predictably, the egocentric Bodenheim looked down on any activity other than his own, and the elderly Hecht was almost as smug and square as young Norman Podhoretz. Out in San Francisco, Kenneth Rexroth—who at his crotchety worst remained more genuinely radical than Hecht or Bogey ever were—blew hot and cold on the issue.[16]

Nelson Algren—a great writer, an important influence on the Beats, and half-Beat himself without realizing it—epitomized the peculiarly uncomprehending attitude toward the Beats on the part of many older radicals when he wrote in 1963: "No investigating committee is ever going to ask anybody, 'Were you ever or are you now a beatnik?'"[17] It would be hard to imagine a more striking example of hitting the nail on the head and still missing it. Like the Hipsters before them, those who came to be called Beatniks had developed new ways of dodging the repressive apparatus, outside traditional organizational and ideological frameworks. The strength of the Beat Generation, as a sinuous and insinuating current of thought and behavior, lay precisely in its ability to evade and avoid the traps set out for one and all by the square world.

The "World Turned Upside-Down" utopianism of the College of Complexes—its insistence on creating a little space for "freedom now," instead of postponing all fun till after the Revolution—predisposed the Janitor and his co-conspirators to the new Beat tremors in the cultural/political atmosphere. Indeed, the College was the vibrant nerve-center of Chicago's Beat movement long before Beat became a term of everyday usage. Today, after nearly thirty years, poet Jack Micheline remembers it warmly: "It was a nice place, jammed full of people, one of the few places in Chicago comparable to the Village in New York, or North Beach in San Francisco—you know, places where people interested in poetry and jazz and things like that could get together and talk."

In the late Fifties, when "beatniks" became the object of a vigorous campaign of hatred and ridicule in movies, popular fiction, newspapers and TV, many bars and coffeehouses all over the country, including Chicago, clamped down and made it known that they had nothing to do with this latest threat to national security. Brundage, however, accepted the challenge; the College served notice that the welcome-mat was out for beatniks of all countries. Indeed, while the more literary Beats of San Francisco, Venice and New York anxiously disowned the abusive "beatnik" label, Brundage and other Collegians flaunted it in the face of the enemy as a badge of honor.

The energy and militancy the College brought to the Cause of Beatdom raised the stakes in the struggle to break out of the Cold War social/cultural stalemate. Having long since superseded the restrictive "political" categories of the traditional Left, Brundage and his co-thinkers were not about to surrender to the retrograde tendencies toward religiosity and neo-patriotism that sometimes passed for Beat. Far more than the orthodox Marxists' endless attempts at "regroupment," or the muddled "mysticism" promoted by a few pontifical Beat celebrities, it was the most uncompromisingly radical forms of Beat disaffiliation, and the defiant pockets of creative freedom they nourished, that inspired the resurgence of mass radicalism in the later Sixties. In this evolution the Janitor and his College were a significant force. Aware that beatdom's journalistic shell was mostly hype and fad, they seized on its radical rank-and-file kernel and went all the way with it. "If you wish to see the so-called 'beat generation' *in action*," wrote syndicated news-columnist Dorothy Kilgallen at the time, "drop into the College of Complexes."[18]

From mid-1958 through the closing of the College in May 1961, Beat activities and polemics dominated *The Curriculum*. Beatnik Poetry Nights, Beatnik Party Nights, Beat plays (notably Jack Gelber's "The Connection"), harangues by Beats and anti-Beats and supporters of Beats were daily affairs. For those who were new to the scene, the College provided its own free *Hipsicon* defining seventy-five Beatnik terms. In 1959 the

College hosted a widely-publicized "Miss Beatnik" competition, spoofing the "Miss America" contest and (not at all incidentally), multiplying enrollment. The winner, Gnomi Gross, was crowned "Queen of the Beatniks" and held forth at the College on "the distaff side of Beatnikism."

Beatnik fervor at the College climaxed in the rise of the Beatnik Party during the 1960 presidential election year. The Party was a pure creation of the College, and Slim Brundage, "leader of all beatniks east of the Mississippi," as a widely reproduced press release described him, was its initiating sparkplug. Its whole point, as he wrote in a letter to Lawrence Ferlinghetti, published in this collection, was "to lampoon the hell out of the powers that be."

The Beatnik Party nominating convention was held July 17–22, 1960 at the College's New York campus, which Brundage had opened at 139 West 10th Street in June 1959. (He had also put down a $10,000 deposit on a place at 638 Broadway in San Francisco's North Beach, but anti-beatnik hysteria on the part of Bay Area real-estate magnates prevented the opening of a College there.) The New York Convention was well-publicized and well-attended. Brundage confided to Ferlinghetti that he himself hoped to be the Party's standard-bearer, and several newspapers ran stories featuring him as the most likely candidate. As it happened, he was not even nominated—definitive proof that the Janitor was no back-room political wheeler-dealer. After much deliberation and delirium, two much younger candidates—or anti-candidates, as they called themselves—were selected: Bill Smith for anti-President, and Joffre Stewart for anti-Vice-President—both from the Chicago delegation, and longtime College regulars.[19]

The Beatnik Party campaign, which surely merits a full-length study, was markedly anarchist and run with zestful humor. "Don't get out the Vote!" was one of its key slogans. The Party platform called for the immediate abolition of government, money and work. Other demands included "Repeal the Federal Narcotics Act" and "making peace with everybody." Some less-appealing inanities were also proposed ("Move the capital of the U.S. from Wall Street to Greenwich Village," etc.), but even these were paragons of wisdom next to the horrifying authoritarianism and militarism that permeated the platforms of the two capitalist parties.

To the Beatnik Party's "Don't Vote" campaign, the U.S. electorate responded with rousing enthusiasm. As with each presidential election since 1936, the percentage of eligible voters who actually bothered to cast ballots declined once again—a clear people's mandate to the victorious Beatniks!

And so, while a rapidly aging Jack Kerouac was babbling about being a Republican and "loving" Eisenhower, and while Allen Ginsberg pursued his unwavering career as loyal Democrat and hence, a "Kennedy man," it was left to Chicago's Beat population to throw pies in the face of America's two-party pseudo-democratic politics.

At the College of Complexes, the Farthest Left of the Far Left also tended to be the Farthest Out of the Far Out.

VII. From the Sixties to the Nineties: A Continuing Education

1959 and '60 were the College's peak years. Largely thanks to the Beatnik craze, and to Brundage's adeptness in identifying it with all that his curriculum stood for, the public image of The Playground for People Who Think grew well beyond its earlier limits. No doubt a few aging cognoscenti continued to relish it as the last fling of the venerable Pickle. Increasingly, however, the College was recognized as the local center for the newest, most original, most audacious and outrageous expressions of cultural and political dissidence. "Everybody at the College was a 'character,' " recalls Ella Jenkins, who was one of them. As a magnet for "characters," the College naturally attracted more and more.

With its irresistible blend of Wobbly/hobo/Dada traditions and youthful Beat-inspired improvisation, The House That Slim Built had evolved into a distinct collectivity with an identity all its own. At no time, before or since, was its internal solidarity or external impact greater than in the glory days of the Beatnik Party anti-presidential campaign. The College's local fame had spread from coast to coast, and was attracting notice abroad. There was even talk of a live College of Complexes TV show.

Incurably "serious" radicals, many of whom had previously

scoffed at its "silliness," now began to view the College as the hottest recruiting-ground in town. As a New York official of the Fair Play for Cuba Committee wrote Slim in 1960, "You are in a good spot to be a liaison between the Committee and young intellectuals and beats."[20] Al Haber, a co-founder of Students for a Democratic Society (SDS), wanted to sign up the sexagenarian Brundage in what would become, a few years later, the largest and most revolutionary student organization in U.S. history.[21] The Janitor's extensive correspondence with such groups, and with many others—including the whole gamut of civil-rights and peace organizations as well as such spokespersons of the Far Left as armed-struggle Black Nationalist Robert F. Williams and the revolutionary pacifist staff of *Liberation* magazine—reveals a man resolved to stay close to everything dynamic, radical and alive. Some of his old friends may have soured on what they now called the "change-the-world racket," but Brundage, albeit no stranger to pessimism himself, always held out a helping hand to sincere radical enemies of the capitalist state.

It was precisely the College's openly oppositional character that served at last to distinguish it from its more traditionally bohemian forebear, the Dil Pickle Club. Unlike Jack Jones, Slim Brundage did his best to provoke the abhorrence, or at least the scorn, of a good part of the mainstream liberal intelligentsia—specifically, the pretentiously "successful" (*i.e.*, commercial) local literati, whose vehement disapproval contributed appreciably to the aura of attractive unrespectability that the College needed to sustain its outsider identity.

Outright squares and pillars of the Establishment—the University of Chicago professors, Congressmen and judges who frequently addressed meetings at the College—were no problem, for no one could confuse such people with the College itself. Indeed, the fact that the College was able to enjoy their services on its own terms added to the appeal (and the humor) of the place. Rather, as targets for their barbs, Brundage and his confrères singled out apologists for censorship, arrogant news-columnists and "hipper-than-thou" *littérateurs* for whom the College was an exasperatingly *gauche* and offensive object worthy only of malicious condescension. Brundage's antipathy to the self-centered erstwhile Pickler Max Bodenheim, and to the

35

then-much-talked-about columnist Jack Mabley (who had fomented the University of Chicago's suppression of a Beat issue of the *Chicago Review*), should be seen in this light. The old romantic slogan *épater le bourgeois* may have seemed *passé*, but bugging the pseudo-hip was still an urgent necessity.

Throughout its Beatnik era, the number of College regulars multiplied, and its periphery, or student body—a melange of weekend beatniks, proto-hippies, and miscellaneous unclassifiable zanies who could be counted on to "spread the word" on College doings—extended all over the city, suburbs and neighboring states. As 1960 drew to a close, the College was clearly a growing force, attracting more and more attention. And because it was a growing *radical* force, and a card-carrying member of the Beatnik Menace to boot, it inevitably also attracted enemies.

In the present state of our knowledge, it is impossible to pinpoint the real reason(s) why the College of Complexes was forced out of business at the very moment that it had begun to prosper far beyond the wildest dreams of its Founding Janitor. Perhaps the answers to this puzzle will be found when and if someone takes the time and trouble to search through whatever remains of Chicago's "Red Squad" files from that period, and Brundage's FBI files as well.

Meanwhile, all we know for sure is that in spring 1961 the United States Internal Revenue Service notified Brundage that the College owed a vast sum in back taxes, payable immediately. Inasmuch as its taxes had always been paid and an I.R.S official had repeatedly assured the College administration that everything was in perfect order, the sudden about-face on the part of the national tax-collection agency seems rather suspect. In any event, Brundage's legal battle against the I.R.S. proved unsuccessful. In March the I.R.S. sold the New York campus for three hundred and sixty dollars. The Chicago original closed in May. Thus Chicago lost its most colorful center of higher learning, and the city's most celebrated Janitor went back to painting houses. As of New Year's Day 1963, Brundage still owed the I.R.S. a total of $101,720.01.

In later years, starting around 1966, Brundage made several attempts to revive the College on a once-a-week basis, meeting in various taverns and restaurants owned by others, but none of these efforts ever caught on. Ironically, throughout the first half of the riotous and revolutionary Sixties, the College was reduced to a memory; and during the second half—apart from a brief August '68 resurgence, at the time of the Democratic Convention protests—it never became more than the faintest shadow of its former rollicking self. A crucial, invaluable momentum had been lost, and Brundage found no way to recover it.

According to Sophie Fagin, one of the first and most insightful historians of Chicago's free-speech forums, such forums tend to proliferate during periods when social conflict is greatest—an observation strongly vindicated during the Sixties and early Seventies. Significantly, however, the forums that developed in those years assumed a wide variety of new forms. Freedom Schools, Be-Ins, Teach-Ins, Free Universities, Women's Liberation Consciousness-Raising Sessions, and Study Groups by the thousand flourished throughout the land. To the young but often quite sophisticated participants in these new forums, the later 1960s and '70s incarnations of the College of Complexes must have seemed quaintly museumlike in comparison. In the days when "Don't Trust Anyone Over Thirty" was a best-selling slogan, how many kids cared about these relics of the Dil Pickle? That the "generation gap" was taking its toll did not escape the Collegians themselves; Fred Thompson, for one, noted wryly that the forum had devolved into little more than "an aggregate of geriatric scissorbills."[22] Even their solid credentials as Wobbly veterans of the Class War and elder anti-statesmen of the Beat Generation brought little glory to Brundage and his soapboxing buddies. The dynamics of the time were such that the young Wob firebrands of the *Rebel Worker* Group—as I can attest, for I was among them—tended to dismiss these old gray heads as "fuddy-duddies." As the Vietnam War escalated, as student radicalism soared from Democratic Party reformism into revolutionary anti-imperialism, as the cry for Black Power went 'round the world, the emphasis everywhere was on action rather than talk.

The still later—and ongoing—post-Brundage revivals of the College have run up against even graver problems: the fragmentation of what was formerly called "The Movement," and all the other dismal consequences of so-called "urban renewal," suburbanization, gentrification, the rise of malls, and the monopolization of the media by multibillionaires—all of which not only coincided with, but contributed to the decline of free speech, the near-annihilation of bohemia and, in turn, the demise of the "public intellectuals" who were, of course, the heart and soul of the College and other places like it. Russell Jacoby's excellent study, *The Last Intellectuals* (1987), despite the author's inexplicable failure even to mention Slim Brundage, sheds an appreciable light on these calamitous developments.

In the face of such unprecedented and self-exacerbating adversities, the College of Complexes bravely persists to this day. In a society that seems to be increasingly made up of passive and inarticulate Spectators of Screens, here is at least one small but implacable oasis of free, open, face-to-face discussion.

VIII. A Historian on the Wrong Side of History

For some fifty years Slim Brundage was "a well-known part of Chicago's network of self-conscious outsiders," as a writer for the *Reader* put it in 1983.[23] Especially after he foisted his raucous College on an unsuspecting public in 1951, his was a name dropped in gossip-columns as well as in coffeehouses, bars, Chinese restaurants, Riccardo's, the Jazz Record Mart, the lobby of the old Clark Theater and everywhere else that radicals and bohemians ran into each other. Once in a while you could catch the Janitor on radio or TV. I remember him one night on Kup's Show, shambling into the room in his rumpled gray outfit, slouching in a chair and scowling at everybody as he railed against one aspect and another of what used to be called "the American Way of Life." As is often the case with curmudgeons, people tended to find him lovable. In 1965 the *Daily News* featured him as one of the sixty-two "Best People" in Chicago.[24]

Even after he retired to Guadalajara, Mexico in 1975 (and to southern California in the late 1980s), Chicagoans remembered Slim Brundage. He kept up quite a correspondence with young friends and old, and often returned during the summer to preside at an occasional College meeting. Long before his death from a brain-hemhorrage at a senior citizens' bingo party in El Centro, California in October 1990, the Janitor had become a fixture of local lore in his old hometown. His well-earned reputation as "Free-Speech Champion" and "cantankerous character" assured him a secure niche in Chicago history. As an "intellectual in the great soapboxer tradition of the anarchists and Wobblies," which is how Jack Micheline remembers him, he had few peers.

That Brundage enjoyed his moments in the limelight can hardly be doubted. The "leader of all beatniks east of the Mississippi" made good copy, which of course always served to attract newcomers to the College. Interestingly, along with IWW songbooks, numerous Charles H. Kerr titles, Haldeman-Julius Little Blue Books and Seymour Krim's anthology, *The Beats*, his library included a well-read manual of press-agentry—a mine of suggestions on how to go about getting the media to promote whatever one happens to be doing.[25] I doubt whether any janitor before or since has ever put such a book to better use.

What Brundage really wanted, however, more than anything else, was to be a writer, and to be accepted as such by other writers. He once said he started scribbling in fifth grade. By the mid-1940s he was writing "like mad" and by the ream. Yearning for recognition as an author, he hired a series of literary agents. Success as a writer, however, continued to elude him. He was unquestionably one of the best known and most prolific authors on Chicago's literary scene, but also one of the least-published. He wrote at least five novels, several autobiographies, a good number of short stories and plays, a few poems, three- or fourscore articles and essays, hundreds of editorials, exhortations and pronunciamentoes, and countless letters to the editor of local and national periodicals. He also compiled several versions of a hobo cookbook. However, aside from his "ravings" in *The Curriculum*, a small fraction of his letters-to-the-editor and an occasional nostalgia-piece in the local press, almost none of this prodigious literary production has ever seen print. All those literary agents seem to have done was to add to his already large collection of rejection-slips.

As Brundage himself admitted in candid moments, he really didn't try very hard at the writing game. He wrote a lot, but couldn't stomach the humiliating ordeal of "trying to get published." After a typescript had been rejected by three or four big publishers, he put it aside and moved on to something else.

Even when he stumbled onto a modicum of success, he rarely followed through. A few of his short plays were performed at the Dil Pickle and the College, but he does not appear to have made any attempt to get them into book-form. The College Archives are rich in his fascinating but uncompleted projects: scripts for radio shows that never were aired; lexicons of IWW and hobo jargon that remain in the 3 x 5 card stage; attempts at anthologies—most notably one of hobo and workingclass songs and poems—left in variously sorry states.

With ninety-five percent of his work unpublished, Brundage's "status" as a writer is clearly a topic for future study. Published or unpublished, his thousands of pages of autobiography will always be an important source for historians of Chicago, labor, free speech, bohemia and the Beat Generation. No doubt, in time, sympathetic explorers of his novels, stories and plays will find that at least some of them possess admirable qualities overlooked by nervous Cold War editors. A few of his playscripts—the early "Skid Road," for example, and one of his last, "Sex And To Hell With Ann Landers"—abound in flashes of dark humor. In the hands of a director with some sense of the Wobbly point of view (I know that's asking a lot), they could be turned into stage-shows or movies worth watching.

His social criticism, too, may turn up material of real value, though in this area he never thought of himself as anything more than a popularizer of other people's ideas. His diatribes against inequality and other facts of life in these United States were merciless, and therefore pertinent, and he had especially interesting things to say on education, free speech and the permanent need for revolt. Some of his short papers, such as his early tribute to Nina Spies and his 1955 "Perspective"—in which he reflects on the relations between humankind and other animals—prefigure themes not widely considered by other radicals till decades later.

Major breakthroughs as an innovative thinker, however, were not Brundage's strong point. For an outspoken defender of the cultural/political radicalism of his time, his grasp of what was happening in poetry, painting, music, film, and critical theory was sadly defective. Despite his best efforts to keep up with Far Left ideas and activity, he remained—to a much greater extent than he himself was aware—a victim of the mass-market middlebrow culture industry. It is discouraging to find him so overawed by mediocre mainstream academics, so deferential to the self-satisfied status-quo intellectual pretensions of the *New York Times* or *The Nation*. It would not be wrong to say that it was Brundage's misfortune to have read Erich Fromm rather than Frantz Fanon and Herbert Marcuse; *The Kinsey Report* rather than Raya Dunayevskaya and James Boggs; Hendrik van Loon and Arthur Schlesinger, Jr., rather than E.P. Thompson and C.L.R. James; Vance Packard rather than Walter Benjamin and André Breton. Sometimes, despairing of finding answers to questions that troubled him, he got caught up in his own Law of Levity. True as it is that whatever comes up for discussion can be brought down with a laugh, life-threatening problems persist.

No two of us are the same, but my own experience convinced me long ago that the best ideas, the most far-reaching insights, always arrive unexpectedly in the course of long, leisurely wandering. The books one reads are not life, and I persist in thinking that Brundage may well have done better to skip the highbrow quotations and the old jokes, relying instead on his own gut-level genius. Less reading of *The Nation*, less respect for top-dollar intellectuals, more long walks, closer attention to the stirrings in the streets: Wouldn't that have helped?

Even with all his limitations, however—limitations he made no effort to conceal—Brundage always held fast to essentials. In stark contrast to the great majority of America's "Left intellectuals" during his lifetime, he remained true to his youthful revolutionary vision of freedom, equality, "a better world." Unlike those who, as Nelson Algren once put it, were on the Left only because of a shortage of jobs on the Right, the Janitor never became an apologist for the system of global misery, murder and terror known as capitalism.

What makes him worth reading is not so much his jaunty prose style, his original ideas, or even his radicalism or humor—though these last two naturally add depth and color to everything he wrote. Slim Brundage is an important writer because he was a lucid, penetrating observer and reporter of the life around him—and what a life it was! The present volume focuses on the

Janitor as a participant-chronicler of Chicago's evolving counter-culture, from the early Twenties through the Sixties. As a modest first-person recorder of the city's subterranean cultural history he is unsurpassed. His short articles, essays and editorial "ravings" on tramping, hobohemia, Bughouse Square, the Dil Pickle, the Beat Generation and his own finest creation, the College of Complexes, seem to me to be his best work as a writer.

In these texts, written in the free-and-easy style of a soapboxer who knows the crowd is with him, Brundage is most thoroughly and happily himself. His purpose, in all of them, is simply to tell the story in his own way. Here and there one can guess at the possible influence of James T. Farrell, Nelson Algren or T-Bone Slim—writers he knew and admired.[26] But his now-you-see-it-now-you-don't way of rambling—a pell-mell of reminiscences, diatribes, digressions, vignettes and one-liners—is 100-proof Brundage.

As a speaker, he was no spellbinder-orator like John Loughman or Charley Wendorf, but even people who didn't like the Janitor conceded his remarkable abilities as a *raconteur*. He knew that a little philosophy goes a long way—and even longer if it is backed up by a little clowning. And thanks to what Burr McCloskey once called his housepainter's "willingness to climb down from the ladder,"[27] he also had a well-developed sense of timing, and a knack for balancing narration, humor and polemic.

Throughout this book his tone is consistently conversational. As a writer of the history he was helping to make, he clearly felt himself to be in constant dialogue with his real and imagined readers who, as he realized, were also making that history and thus, in a sense, helping him write it. Indeed, many of these texts originally appeared in *The Curriculum*, which he edited, and which was read by everyone who had anything to do with the College.

Brundage makes us aware that the hobohemian free-speech forum culture—the world of the IWW, Bughouse Square, the Hobo College, the Dil Pickle Club, the College of Complexes and their allied publishing houses and bookshops—is a unique and invaluable part of America's subversive heritage. He makes us realize, too, that the influence of this hobohemia—on individual workers and on the whole local labor movement as well as on writers, artists, revolutionists, intellectuals—has been enormous, and has by no means reached the end of the line.

Reading these texts, one is astonished to realize how little of substance has been written on this subject elsewhere. What little has been published about it consists almost entirely of anecdotes in long-out-of-print memoirs. I think this paucity of information astonished Brundage, too, and finally made him resolve to fill the breach. As a lifelong insider of an outsider society, he was certainly well-qualified to be its eyewitness historian. Brundage tells anecdotes, too—and some of the best— but he also offers us the fullest, most coherent account of the whole countercultural community.

Of course there are oversights and omissions. Many important matters are hastily glossed over. Brundage is often agonizingly brief precisely where we would have liked him to take the time to tell us more. Of the historical articles collected here, there is hardly one that would not have been improved by doubling or tripling the amount of detail.

And yet, more than anyone else, the Janitor conveys a real sense of what it was like to be a part of the extraordinary community he is writing about. He opens doors to places long gone, turns the lights back on and invites us in for a drink. He introduces us to his old friends: the Pickle's irascible Jack Jones, with whom he quarreled; hobofeminist-socialist "Red Martha" Biegler; Bughouse Square's Dave Tullman, John Loughman and the "Cosmic Kid"; Hobo College chairman Jack Macbeth; guitar-playing "Clark Street" Mary Riley, and many other figures of nobility and charm. Systematically overlooked by small-minded biographers of the officially "great," every one of these amazing unknowns deserves a place in a new *Arabian Nights*. Brundage wants us to meet them not only because he knew them in their prime, but also because he never forgot how much they meant to him, and to his world. He is convinced, moreover, and hopes to convince us, that these people, the lives they lived, the wonders they accomplished on less than a shoestring—their marvelous *example*, in a word—are important for us, too, and for our world, and for the future.

These historical "ravings," in short, are the best personal narrative of what may well be the oldest continuous and self-renewing radical counterculture in this country.

Continuous? Well, yes, strange as it may seem. True, these are hard times for free spirits, and only a few small remnants of this once vast, sprawling community are still trying to "hold the fort." But in view of the terrifying thoroughness with which this country's repressive apparatus tends to obliterate all radical opposition, the fact that anything at all survives of the old hobohemia is practically a miracle. And yet, in spite of everything, a few recalcitrants of the College of Complexes still assemble for weekly meetings, the IWW maintains a Chicago office and meets monthly, and even Bughouse Square comes alive with speakers—once a year. And as the book you are now reading demonstrates, the Charles H. Kerr Company—world's oldest publisher of anti-Establishment literature—is still very much in the game.

How did Chicago's blue-collar counterculture manage to hold out, when its counterparts around the country disintegrated decades ago? The answer is simple: It survived because it never succumbed to "Success," never allowed itself to be absorbed into the exploitative system. Few things are sadder than a once-radical institution that has become domesticated, "commercially viable" and respectable, embraced by the very Order it formerly and bravely stood against. Self-immunized against the delusion of "making it" within the framework of the existing social set-up, Chicago's hobohemia never became a saleable commodity. Brundage often refers to the College regulars as "pseudo-intellectuals"; he even titled a paper on the place "The Last Refuge of the Pseudo-Intellectual." The term is unfortunate and misleading, for he did not mean to imply that his friends were charlatans or *poseurs*, but simply that they did not in fact make their living as intellectuals. Such people could more accurately be termed amateur intellectuals, or non-commercial public intellectuals—people whose *thought* is *not for sale*. Many decades before Hipsters and Beats made "selling out" their deadliest accusation and insult, Wobblies and other radical labor activists used the same term to denounce those in their ranks who made their peace with Capital.

Brundage and his impossible College exemplified this hobohemian variant of what Herbert Marcuse, following André

Breton, called The Great Refusal: the refusal to accept the rules of a game in which the dice are loaded. Brundage had no kick against making a buck, but it had to be on his terms, and his terms never conformed to the profiteers' code.

A writer once said of Brundage: "He has failed so often that failure has made him free."[28] The Janitor's failures were many: Above all, he failed to renounce the ideals of his youth, to make a lot of money, to buy himself a comfortable position in the ruling class. These also happen to be the "failures" of the IWW, the anarchists, small-c communists, Hipsters and Beats.

Compared to the unrelieved horror known as "Success," this kind of "failure" is rich with promise, ablaze with all the possibilities of tomorrow.

In response to the self-satisfied pseudo-Marxist hacks of yesteryear, who blathered that "History is on our side," Brundage regarded himself unequivocally as "a man on the wrong side of history."[29] Resolutely minoritarian, against-the-current, out of the running, he identified with those who truly have nothing to lose. His old-time Wobbly solidarity—what Meta Toerber calls his "profound empathy for the underdogs of the world"—remained steadfast to the end. A grafitti on the College wall defined him as "the kind of guy who would sit on a barrel of scotch in a harem and complain." For him, fanning the flames of discontent was as natural as breathing. He called himself "a foreigner in his own country" and, no less revealingly, "the luckiest man alive."[30] Life on the margins—the only life he knew or wanted—had its risks and woes, but also its supreme joys.

Looking back on his eighty-odd years of misadventures, he concluded that his was "a life well-spent. What wasn't well-spent was loaned out," he added, "and somebody still owes me for it."[31] He was right: Everyone who cares for freedom and a better world owes something to Slim Brundage.

Franklin Rosemont

Chicago, Groundhog Day 1997

NOTES

1. This historical sketch of the College of Complexes and the life of Slim Brundage is based chiefly on materials in the extensive College of Complexes Archives, henceforth cited in these notes as the College Archives. (For a brief description of these Archives, see "Sources," at the end of this volume.)

The College Archives have not been catalogued and, for the time being, are not available to researchers. Many typescripts, moreover, exist in multiple variants, making citation difficult. In this introduction, therefore, I have kept notes to a minimum, citing sources primarily for otherwise unidentified quoted passages.

Books and articles consulted in the course of this project are listed in the Bibliography.

2. Karl Marx, letter to Arnold Ruge, September 1843. See "Letters from the *Deutsch-Franzoische Jahrbucher*," in Karl Marx and Frederick Engels, *Collected Works* (New York: International Publishers, 1975), III: 142.

3. *A Salute to the Janitor*, an unpaginated 16-page memorial pamphlet prepared by Burr McCloskey and others in November 1990, shortly after Brundage's death.

4. Note that this discussion occurred in 1952, four years after the publication of Norman Mailer's *The Naked and the Dead* but nine years before the appearance of Joseph Heller's *Catch-22*.

5. The name of the Dil Pickle Club was originally spelled Dill, with two l's, but one l was soon dropped, allegedly to avoid a trademark dispute. Pickle publications, however, were not always consistent in this regard, and secondary literature on the subject almost invariably spells it with two l's.

The Pickle's history, especially its early period, is shrouded in obscurity. Many are the impressionistic accounts of the Club and its doings, but practically every one of them disagrees on important points with all the others. See Bibliography.

6. From 1928 through 1941, Thompson spent several months a year teaching Marxist economics and labor history at the IWW's Work People's College in Duluth, Minnesota.

7. The Council and its activities thus far seem to have been overlooked by labor historians. The College Archives include a substantial file of correspondence, publications and clippings on the subject.

8. Slim Brundage, "Non-heretical Heretic," undated typescript (*circa* late 1940s), in the College Archives.

9. Quoted in a photocopied mock-up of a prospectus, prepared by Burr McCloskey, for a proposed omnibus volume of Brundage's writings; this prospectus accompanies McCloskey's 2 July 1990 letter to Brundage, in the College Archives.

10. *Ibid.*

11. Burr McCloskey, "The High Price of Free Speech" (see Bibliography).

12. The role of the forums in providing respite from racism, and in actively promoting struggle against racism, has been largely ignored by historians. Participants' accounts, however, offer moving testimony in this regard. In her fascinating memoirs, the African American and Montauk Indian poet, playwright and educator Olivia Ward Bush-Banks (1869–1944) fondly recalled her years at Chicago's Abraham Lincoln Center, founded by socialist Jenkin Lloyd Jones: "What a flood of memories come over me as I think of the weekly Friday morning Forum, when I listened to men and women of national and international repute from every part of the Globe. How these messages burned their way deep into my very soul! And, always the noon-hours proved a happy climax when we enjoyed the pleasant experience of dining together. There I discovered real comrades, whose friendship remained true thro' the years. . . . Best of all, the Center inspired me with its genuine spirit of comradeship towards all individuals and groups, regardless of nationality or condition." See *The Collected Works of Olivia Ward Bush-Banks* (in Bibliography), 284–285.

13. Robert Weinberg, "Cover Art in *Weird Tales*," in his *WT50: A Tribute to Weird Tales* (Oak Lawn, IL: Robert W. Weinberg, 1974), notes that Margaret Brundage's first

Weird Tales cover appeared in September 1932. From mid-1933 to the end of '38 "Mrs Brundage was to dominate *WT* cover art. . . . When one thinks of *Weird Tales* covers, one first thinks of Margaret Brundage." Over half the article is devoted to her covers.

14. For example, Jean Toomer's aphorism: "Aim to use insanity as a means of developing reason"—from his *Essentials* (Chicago, Private Edition, 1931).

15. Sympathetic articles on the Beat Generation did appear in a few Left publications, notably the *Industrial Worker, Liberation* and (occasionally) *Dissent.*

16. Rexroth's widely reprinted 1957 essay, "Disengagement: The Art of the Beat Generation," was militantly pro-Beat. But as Morgan Gibson remarks in his *Revolutionary Rexroth*, "His support of the Beat movement was critical and temporary" (see Bibliography), 22.

17. Nelson Algren, *Who Lost An American?* (New York: Macmilan, 1963), 283. See also my " 'Reckless Politics in Chicago': Nelson Algren and Louis Lingg," in Roediger and Rosemont, eds., *Haymarket Scrapbook* (see Bibliography), 239.

18. Undated (early spring 1960) clipping in the College Archives. Although Kilgallen was referring to the College's New York campus, her remarks apply even more to the Chicago original.

19. William Lloyd Smith (1924–1995) was the College's most frequent speaker. Manager for a time of "Maury's Beatnik Bookstore" on North State Street in the 1950s, he later ran the College's own in-house bookstore. A photo of Smith at the Beatnik Party Convention in New York appears in Fred McDarrah, *Kerouac and His Friends* (see Bibliography), 171.

Born in 1925, Joffre Stewart renounced his citizenship and declared himself a stateless person on Nagasaki Day 1950. Anarchopacifist, poet and "Advocate of the Anti-Christ," he is one of the "characters" in Allen Ginsberg's *Howl* (the one "who reappeared on the West Coast investigating the F.B.I. in beards and shorts with big pacifist eyes sexy in their dark skin passing out incomprehensible leaflets"). He is also described and quoted at length in Lawrence Lipton's *Holy Barbarians* (see Bibliography), 301–305. Stewart's *Poems and Poetry* was brought out by the Now and Then Publishing Cooperative in Voorheesville, New York, in 1982, and he is still active in Chicago's poetry scene.

20. Undated letter from Pat Linden, of the Fair Play for Cuba Committee in New York, to Slim Brundage, in a 1960 correspondence file in the College Archives.

21. Postcard from Al Haber to Slim Brundage, in a 1960 correspondence file in the College Archives.

22. Thompson's quip was relayed to me by Carlos Cortez.

23. Lee Sustar, "When Speech Was Free" (see Bibliography), 16.

24. *Chicago Daily News Panorama*, cover feature, 31 July 1965.

25. Charles Washburn, *Press-Agentry* (New York: National Library Press, 1937), which includes chapters on "Ballyhooing" and "Stunts."

26. A friend of Brundage's from Dil Pickle days, Farrell was active in the affairs of the College's New York campus.

The Janitor's admiration for Algren survived a mid-1950s rift after Algren snubbed a College event in his honor; see his open letter to Algren in *The Curriculum* (July 1956), 2. On T-Bone Slim, see Brundage's "Hobo Colleges," below. Texts by T-Bone Slim figure in at least one of Brundage's 1940s plays, and in his 1980s projected anthology of hobo verse.

27. Quoted in *A Salute to the Janitor, op cit.*

28. Terri Schultz, "King of Failures Clings to his 'College' Presidency," *Chicago Tribune*, 21 July 1972.

29. "Ravings," *The Curriculum* (November 1960), 4.

30. Quoted in McCloskey's prospectus, as described in Note 9 above. *The Luckiest Man Alive* is the title of Brundage's last and longest autobiography, now in Special Collections at Newberry Library.

31. *Ibid.*

A NOTE ON THE TEXTS

THIS BOOK IS DIVIDED into two sections. The first collects Slim Brundage's writings on the history of Chicago's hobohemia and its interaction with both the revolutionary workers' movement and radical/bohemian intellectual currents. The second presents a selection of his more philosophical exhortations, most of them editorials from *The Curriculum*, the official publication of the College of Complexes. This bipartite division notwithstanding, the reader is guaranteed to find a lot of philosophizing and editorializing in the historical articles, and more than a little history in the editorials.

Like all good storytellers, the Janitor told the same stories over and over, but never the same way twice. As a writer he frequently covered the same ground in more than one text, and later borrowed elements from one text to elaborate another.

He was well aware that he needed an editor. As he once put it in a letter to me, he especially wanted someone to go over his work and "take out the redundancies."

The historical essays have been selected from the voluminous and mostly unpublished writings in the College of Complexes Archives. I have arranged them in roughly chronological order according to topic (rather than date of composition). Many of these texts exist in two, three or even more versions, often written at long intervals. Some were evidently expanded with a hope of publication in mind, and others chopped down to fit into the monthly *Curriculum*. Since no two versions contain exactly the same information, and since the purpose of this book is to bring together as much as possible of Brundage's writings on Chicago's hobohemian counterculture, I have freely combined two or more versions of an essay, and sometimes have incorporated additional pertinent matter from other texts.

The Janitor's "Ravings"—his editorials in *The Curriculum*—present similar problems, for many of them turn out to be excerpts from larger unpublished pieces, hurriedly abridged and revised for immediate publication. In such cases, the texts published here are generally based on the larger originals, but include those revisions which add substantially to the text's informational value. At the end of the book is a brief key to the specific sources of each text.

Apart from combining certain texts—a procedure made relatively easy by the Janitor's digressive "That-reminds-me" style—I have edited lightly, desiring at all costs to retain what Carl Sandburg once called Brundage's "pure Americanese. . . a lingo that sings." What changes I have made have been mostly for the sake of clarity, and of course to "take out the redundancies."

The reader should bear in mind that Brundage wrote most of these articles from memory, with little or no documentation at hand. Many dates and other details have proved impossible to verify. Here and there, to help fill in the story, I have added a transitional sentence or phrase, and some explanatory notes.

The typescript of Brundage's last, longest, most complete autobiography may be consulted at Newberry Library. An important and informative memoir, it adds a mass of details to the topics discussed in the articles gathered here. In the hope that it will be published some day in its entirety, I have refrained from excerpting it for the present collection.

Two stylistic points:

1) As Brundage himself explains in "Memoirs of a Dil Pickler" (see also Note 5 to the Introduction), Dil with one l is the correct spelling of the famous Chicago hobohemian nightspot of the 1920s. This may be a hopelessly lost cause—scholars and journalists seem incapable of using a "wrong" spelling, even when it's correct—but I have retained the correct one-l spelling here out of respect for Brundage, who always insisted on it.

2) Brundage regularly wrote "janitor" after his signature, usually with a lower-case j. In this book, however, when referring to him by that distinguished title, I have used a cap J.

As Burr McCloskey once wrote: "All honor to Slim Brundage!"

F.R.

Sam Ball addressing Jack Macbeth's hobo college, the Social Science Institute (c. 1937)

I.

FREE SPEECH
IN THE HEARTLAND

CONTRIBUTIONS
TO THE HISTORY
OF CHICAGO'S
RADICAL
WORKINGCLASS
COUNTERCULTURE

Slim Brundage and friend, around the time of The Knowledge Box (1937)

ALL YOU NEED TO KNOW
ABOUT SLIM BRUNDAGE

Editor's Note: *This autobiographical sketch predates the 1951 opening of the College of Complexes by five or six years.*

* * *

BORN NOVEMBER 29, 1903. . . Insane asylum, Blackfoot, Idaho. . .Whether conception was by accident or design is not a matter of record. . . Dubbed Myron Reed Brundage by misguided parents. . . Named after a renegade Methodist preacher who taught the Bible according to Karl Marx. . . Said renegade often got himself in trouble. . . So did his namesake. . . Forever after. . .

Male progenitor was newspaperman at times. . . The one-man kind: editor, typesetter, makeup man, pressman, salesman and newsboy. . . Radical. . . Trying to make a living running a one-man weekly in Idaho would make anybody radical. . . In 1912 he worked on the campaign to elect Eugene V. Debs President of the United States on the Socialist ticket. . . He gave up newspapering. . . Got a nice easy job digging ditches. . . in between revolutions. . .

Mother worked in bughouse. . . Hailed from St. Cloud, Minnesota. . . Died at age twenty-eight (I was seven). . . Father raised three boys. . . More or less. . . Nobody else would have us. . . Put me in Norwegian orphans' home at ten. . . Didn't like the place. . . Stirred up minor rebellion against poor food and restriction of privileges. . . Told the other kids not to say their prayers. . . The heads hollered that Pop should take me out before I wrecked the morale of the joint. . . He did. . .

Went to work on a farm for board and room. . . Pulling teats on heifers. . . Also a little gardening. . . Potatoes, cabbages, kale, carrots, stromberries. . . Row on row. . . Mile on mile. . . Allergic to gardens ever since. . .

Newsboy on battleships at twelve. . . Pinsetter. . . Building laborer. . . Driller's helper in Navy Yard, Bremerton, Wash. . . Dishwasher in beanery, Olympia, Wash. . . Whistle-punk for logging crew. . .

Depression in 1920. . . Occupation: hobo. . . Farm hand

again. . . Hobo some more. . . Chaingang convict, vagrancy, El Paso, Texas. . . Wore hobbles. . . Hobo some more. . . Harvest hand. . . Fruitpicker and horsedung spreader in California. . . Hobo some more. . .

In Gulfport, Mississippi, picked up the first tool that ever fit my hand: a paint brush. . . Started working as painter. . .

Chaingang some more, St Augustine, Florida. . . No chains this time. . . Nice clothes, but the stripes ran the wrong way. . . Thirty days. . . Hobo some more. . . Building laborer, Nashville, Tenn. . . Painter again. . . Roadbuilder and dishwasher. . . Building laborer. . . Furniture-and piano-mover. . . Painter on swingstage. . . Bouncer at Dil Pickle Club. . . Soapboxer at Bug Club and Bughouse Square. . . County jail convict. . . Speakeasy operator. . . Bohemian joint operator. . . Hobo Forum operator. . . Painting contractor. . . Decorator. . . Steel painter. . . Pipe painter. . . Hobo College operator. . . Now president emeritus of that institution. . . Swingstage painter. . . Novelist (I hope). . . As yet unpublished. . .

Joined first union at age of fourteen. . . Boilermakers, Bremerton. . . Joined Wobblies (Industrial Workers of the World) at sixteen, Aberdeen, Wash. . . Joined Painters' Union (American Federation of Labor) at twenty-two, Chicago. . . Late 1930s, attended meetings of the Revolutionary Workers' League. . . Secretary of Religion and Labor Foundation. . . Organized Council for Union Democracy in 1943. . . Same is small but effective. . . Object: to clean up corrupt unions. . .

Marital mistakes. . . Two-time loser. . . First time, Margaret. . . Half Swede, half Orkney Islander. . . Commercial artist. . . Did covers for *Weird Tales*. . . One brat. . . Nineteen. . . Now on oil-can between Iran and Singapore. . .

Second offense Katherine. . . Perennial student. . . B.A. in Latin, U. of Missouri. . . M.A. in Greek. . . Cornell. . . Studied drama under Baker, Yale. . . Law at DePaul, Chicago. . . One more brat. . . Dubbed Steamboat. . . One dog, Menace. . . She barks, that's all. . .

Now painting El structure on New Lots line, New York. . . Kid stuff. . . Too damned old. . . Can't take it. . . Got to. . . Had a fight with Painters' Union bureaucrats in Manhattan. . . Steel painters don't belong to Council, so can work there. . .

Stuck hand in suction fan in 1927. . . Lost two fingers and damaged hand fifty percent. . . Fell thirty-five feet in 1940, while painting smokestack. . . Broke back and ankle. . . Thought I'd die. . . Docs found arrested TB scar tissue. . . Half of lungs. . . Other ailments: nervous indigestion, insomnia, dandruff, fallen arches, falling teeth, failing eyes, falling apart. . . Diagnosis of my friends: hypochondria. . .

Started school at six: too dumb. . . Started again at seven: too smart. . . Always in trouble. . . Seven and a half years in school. . . Twenty-four teachers. . . Tried several schools since. . . Allergic to instruction. . .

Started writing in fifth grade. . . Latest wife sent me to night-school to learn where to start and stop a sentence. . . Still don't know. . . Had my first play performed in the Dil Pickle in 1928. . . Written several since. . . Member of Chicago Repertory Group, 1938. . . Tried writing verse, soap operas, short stories, essays, tracts—everything but music. . . Never published anything that I got paid for. . . Never tried very hard. . .

And now, first try at a novel. . . .

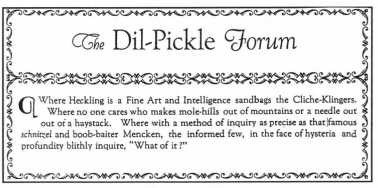

The Dil-Pickle Forum

Where Heckling is a Fine Art and Intelligence sandbags the Cliche-Klingers. Where no one cares who makes mole-hills out of mountains or a needle out out of a haystack. Where with a method of inquiry as precise as that famous *schnitzel* and boob-baiter Mencken, the informed few, in the face of hysteria and profundity blithly inquire, "What of it?"

From a Dil Pickle Club flyer (1920s)

TRAMPING: A LOST TRADITION
Or, What Has Happened to Our Hoboes?

DURING THE EARLY DAYS of the Great Depression the homeguards of California tried to get a law passed to keep tramps out of the state. In response, a howl of protest went up from all nine hundred miles of its length. Some of the biggest names in the state, including the publisher of the *Los Angeles Times*, said "Man, I came into this country on top of a box-car."

That condition was not indigenous to California alone. Back in those days there seemed to be a glamour attached to the Road. Jack London, Jim Tully, Harry Kemp and many others wrote popular books about tramping. A Chicago judge told me how he used to hobo down to the harvest fields to work while he was on vacation from college.

One time I was taken off the blinds of a passenger train down in Florida. Riding in the back seat of the flivver with me was one of the town boys about my age. He whispered, "My name is Willy Outlaw. This deputy sheriff is a fee grabber. He ran out of booze and told me that if I could find a tramp on that train he'd get enough off the sheriff to buy another bottle. If he delivers you to the county seat you'll get sixty days in the hoosegow."

"What are you putting me wise for?" I asked.

"I been around a little myself," he answered.

That was enough to say: He had been there and he was one of the fraternity. I took his word for it and lit out on high when we pulled up in front of the jail. The deputy emptied his gun at me, but we figured he was too drunk to hit anything so I kept on running. Next morning I dinged the highway out of town.

Probably half the boys in the small town I was raised in went on the road sometime before they were grown. It was a tradition. Their parents had migrated there from places a long way off. Were we going to stay there and become homeguards without ever having seen anything of the world?

The same thing that makes juvenile delinquents today was what made us tick way back then. In some way we had to prove we were men. This has been the way of boys as long as written history and maybe a million years before. In many primitive tribes there are some pretty rugged maturity rites to initiate the youth into manhood. Maybe it was the same thing with us.

Or maybe it was a way of working out our aggressions. Today the kids may be doing the same thing with their drag races, muggings, burglaries, and other rebellions against the status quo. Maybe it was a release from the discipline of school, farm, parents, or just the work and responsibility we knew we were going to be saddled with the rest of our lives. As one ex-hobo put it, "now I'm wearing a hole in the sidewalk from my job to my bed."

Possibly, if the ex-bo told the truth, he would be like the veteran of the last war who said, "It's an experience I'm glad I had, but I don't want to live through it again."

Forty-five years ago I dinged the Mission in Yuma, Arizona. After I put away a meal big enough for two men the boss put me to work. After about an hour he stopped me. Handing me a coin he said, "Here's two bits to chew on."

Only an ex-bo knows how to put words together like that.

General William Tecumseh Sherman said if he owned hell and Texas, he'd live in hell and rent out Texas. I agree. A miserable country breeds miserable people. I've got the scars to prove it.

In 1920, when I was sixteen, I'd been working in Yuma, Arizona. When I got to El Paso, I wasn't prepared for the Texas treatment. I went down to the border and asked an official in khaki how to get over to Juarez. He took me up to court instead. The cop admitted that I didn't try to mooch him, but the judge concluded: "Just plain bum. We'd better detain him a few days." I didn't know then that this was against the Constitution, but I guess knowing it wouldn't have mattered much anyway.

Of all the jail-time I ever did, this Texas chaingang was the worst. Every morning they hobbled my legs with padlocks half as big as my fist. We worked on the road each day for ten hours. When they hauled us back to jail the first day, both of my ankles were raw. Then another con showed me how to hook wire (from the chain and to my belt) to take the strain off of my ankles.

The chaingang experience taught me to stay away from Texas.

But tramping must have had a popular appeal or so many writers wouldn't have used it as a theme. Jack London must have been a real tramp. His book, *The Road*, is full of a lot of guck, but he knew what he was talking about. Romantic prevarication is as necessary to being a successful fictioneer as it is to being a successful dingbat.

London was always talking about honest labor but there isn't much evidence he stayed too close to the work bit. However, he sure does a bang-up job of telling what a dingbat he was. According to him, he was always telling women at back doors how he was trying to get to his rich sister in San Diego. He told this story so many times he began to believe it.

In the literature of the road there are also a lot of phonies. Harry Kemp's *Tramping on Life* was a best-seller forty-five years ago. He says he got on a box-car in El Paso and four hours later he was in Pratt, Kansas. That rattler must have had wings, for that's about four hundred miles through the mountains. In those days the Golden State Limited averaged thirty miles an hour.

Another character who made a good thing out of being a 'bo was Dr Ben Reitman, who ran the world's most successful Hobo College here in Chicago—back in the 1920s.

I once gave a series of tests to a bunch of alleged 'boes to determine how many weren't just scissorbills. Reitman didn't know a shack from a sandhouse or a con from a town clown. If he had to rustle a stew down in the jungles he wouldn't even know how to build the fire. Under pressure he broke down and admitted he was nothing but a circus tramp.

Now no self-respecting 'bo needs a circus to get him around the country. Or to eat, either.

There's no telling how many men forty years ago spent part of their youth tramping. There must have been millions. I've met them in many kitchens behind the back doors I begged. I've met them on farms and in factories, in executive offices, in politics, and even behind a pulpit.

Working construction makes a person fatalistic. At seventeen I worked for Ben Fox in Nashville for twenty cents an hour. His carpenter, who took me home to dinner, introduced me to *The Rubaiyat of Omar Khayyam.* The verse I learned that day stuck with me:

> *Oh, threats of hell and hopes of paradise*
> *One thing is certain, this life flies.*
> *One thing is certain and the rest is lies,*
> *The flower that once has blown forever dies.*

When I got to Cairo, Illinois, a crew was painting the bridge across the Ohio River. I asked for the job. "Are you a high man or a low man?" the foreman asked. "High," I said (I'd never worked on a bridge before). He put me on top girder.

I bummed my way to Chicago where I stayed at Old Lady Grant's Rooming House—that's what the bums called Grant Park, on Chicago's lakefront. Omar grows on you like a dope habit. So I bought a second-hand copy of *The Rubaiyat* on my first Chicago payday.

Did Omar change my life? No. I saw his verse as a record of things as they are.

Before the journalism schools invaded the newspapers there were a lot of tramp reporters dinging around the country. Tramp cooks, tramp printers, tramp railroaders and building mechanics were common. These men were also called boomers. They were unmarried and restless. Usually they had a few bucks and were on their way to another town for a job. A union card was good for a free pass on any rattler most of the time.

But being a railroad bum in the 1920s was a hard life. To catch a train on the fly, we ran alongside to match its speed. Once I grabbed for the rung, hit a pile of tiles, and sprawled all over the roadbed. Damn wonder I lived through it.

Sometimes even the shacks (railroad guards) took pity. That night when I caught the Golden State Limited out of Chicago, it was sub-zero weather. Less than a hundred miles out, the boss shack flashed his light up and said, "Get down." I got down. He looked me over.

"Look at the miserable son of a bitch," he said. "Half frozen." He put me in an empty mail car and I rode to California in style.

When I was shagged out of Redding, California, another tall skinny guy (more uncouth than I, if that's possible) attached himself to me. He wanted to rob every farmhouse we passed. I objected. "Those are working people and they had to work for everything they have," I said. I never convinced him.

The radical labor union I belonged to, the Industrial Workers of the World (IWW), believed in sharing among workfolk. But petty thieves on the bum were just petty thieves. Even on the chaingang, convicts stick together.

Sometimes even cops had a heart. In Los Angeles, when I hit a well-dressed man for a handout, he handed me fifty cents, showed me his shield and said: "Watch yourself, kid. *Some* of these cops will run you in."

Perhaps the day of the chronic dingbat is not over. It's been so many years since I jungled up, I wouldn't know. Years ago I saw a fire in a culvert in northern California. Beside it was a dingbat eighty years old. His beard covered his chest and it was as black as the Chicago subway when all the lights go out. He'd been on the bum since he left County Kilkenny sixty-five years before. That El Paso judge who sentenced me to ten days on the chaingang called me, "just plain bum"—that was this fellow's status, too, but with him it was chronic.

The most charming of all the chronic bums I knew was Deacon Budman. He used to say, "You bums are Johnnie-come-latelies. It wasn't the depression of '29 that put me on the stem. It wasn't '21 or '14 or '07. I've been unemployed since the panic of 1893."

Another gag he used to get off was how the begging profession was deteriorating. "It used to be a dingbat had to have some talent in mooching the stem or dinging the privates. Now all a bum has to do is talk the caseworker out of a new pair of shoes."

The Deacon got his name because he passed his hat in open forums all the way from Boston Commons to the beach of Nome, Alaska. He shacked up in one of Jack London's cabins for over a year. When Mrs London asked Jack why he didn't throw Budman out like he did the many other guests who over-stayed their welcome, he replied, "I hope to get a book out of him."

There is a definition which the stiffs are fond of using, but which isn't always correct. It goes like this: "A hobo is a migratory worker. A tramp is a migratory non-worker. A bum is a non-migratory non-worker." But boomers are called tramp-this and tramp-that, while they are really hoboes according to that definition. All of them are called bums or stiffs sometimes, even by themselves. And there were few of them who didn't do some work at least, sometime.

Morris Budman was one of the few. He would go to prodigious effort to avoid anything that had an odor of honest labor to it. All he ever knew as a child was work. His parents were poverty-stricken immigrants from Russia. Even when the family got a store of their own he worked day and night. It built in him a repugnance he just couldn't live down.

Dave Tullman had degenerated into a town bum by the time I knew him. He was always bragging about how he could make a living without working. The State Department ordered him deported to England—a very grave injustice on account of he "never done nothing." The Snivel Liberties Union fought his case for two years, but the State Department decided he'd lived here long enough doing nothing—he could go back home and do nothing over there the rest of his life. (He writes that the dole ain't so bad.)

About ten percent of the stiffs I met on the road fell into this category. They were either chronic loafers or criminals. One tramp told me he'd made up his mind he'd never make the stir again when he'd gotten out last time. Now he wasn't so sure. We were hungry and cold. And he just couldn't see that job stuff. "What's the difference between the pen and that factory? Nothing but the streetcar ride."

What has happened to our hoboes? Have we urbanized so much? Was this tradition part of small-town America? Do today's youth have more rewarding outlets? Is it the army or the automobile? Is it the vanished frontier or the caseworker which is turning this new youth to other adventures? Is it because we are getting better educations or because there are more women around? Or is it, as Vance Packard postulates, that we are becoming a nation of status-seekers and there just ain't no status no more in being a 'bo?

I don't know. But I'd rather have my kid sleeping in culverts alongside some jungle fire than putting the arm on some helpless old man on a dark street. At one back door I dinged in Memphis the lady said, "Oh my, I guess we better give him something. He's willing to ask for it rather than steal it."

AN OLD-TIME WOBBLY SPEAKS OUT

THE GREATEST FIGHT for free speech in the history of the United States was that of the Wobblies in the 1910s and early '20s. Their free-speech fights are an epic in American culture. Up and down the Pacific Coast states the IWW was agitating for the One Big Union. As word went out, Wobs would rally at the town where the fight centered. As fast as one soapboxer was dragged off to jail, another would mount the box and continue the fight. They filled the jails. But they won clean bunkhouses and decent food from then on in all the logging camps. I know, I worked in them.

Big Bill Haywood, Ralph Chaplin, Vincent St John and many other Wobblies went to jail for sedition for opposing World War I. They were not pacifists. As Fred Thompson said in the College of Complexes, "We just object to one working man going out and killing another working man just to defend some capitalist's money."

In my youth in 1919 I was a member and organizer for the Wobblies. They were just what they claimed to be: the Industrial Workers of the World. By only one week did I miss the Centralia, Washington shootout, for which a number of Wobblies went to prison for fourteen years.

The Wobblies are probably the most effective group of revolutionists the United States has ever turned out. They do not believe you can lick the capitalists at the ballot box. They believe in direct action. They say the field of battle is the job. They have probably gained more for the people they represent than any workers' organization extant.

Some time ago I attended a rally addressed by the Great White Hope of all Communists. Comrade Browder got up and gave a nice little political speech. It wasn't as good as any second-rate soapboxer could deliver, but it was as good as most Aldermen could do. He said: Hooray for the New Deal! Hooray for Abraham Lincoln! Hooray for the Communist Party! And he said that all Democrats are swell fellows except this guy Martin Dies.

A nice little political speech—but I couldn't find anything revolutionary in it. He didn't say anything about helping the working class, or abolishing the capitalist system. He said President Roosevelt is a swell guy and everybody ought to give him a vote. Of course this guy Roosevelt has said time and again that all he wanted to do is make capitalism work. So does Browder.

The Communist Party is not revolutionary and not working class. It is a slightly pink outfit of middleclass malcontents who advocate a totalitarian form of society.

As an old-time Wobbly, I have nothing but contempt for these middle-class, non-revolutionary, so-called "Communists."

Now here are some excerpts from the IWW Preamble:

> *The working class and the employing class have nothing in common. There can be no peace so long as hunger and want are found among millions of working people and the few, who make up the employing class, have all the good things of life.*

> *Between these two classes a struggle must go on until the workers of the world organize as a class, take possession of the earth and the machinery of production, and abolish the wage system.*

That is what revolution means to me. That's what my mother gave me with her milk. That's what I've gone to jail for. That's what I've seen other men spend twenty years of their life for.

Incidentally, the slogan I sign off all my letters with— "Yours for a Better World"—I borrowed from the Wobblies. They were using it during the First World War, if not earlier.

On November 11 (Armistice Day) 1919, a mob of armed American Legionnaires attacked the IWW hall in **Centralia**, Washington, and lynched IWW member Wesley Everest. Early in the attack, several Wobs fired back in self-defense. After a trial long since universally regarded as one of the most notorious frame-ups in U.S. history, seven IWW members were convicted of second-degree murder and sentenced to long prison terms. (No lynchers were tried.) Six members of the jury later gave affidavits stating that they would have voted to acquit had they known the facts in the case. ¶ A Communist since 1919, **Earl Browder** (1891–1973) became Party secretary in 1930, and its presidential candidate in 1936 and 1940. During his long regime, U.S. Communists became indissolubly tied to the Democratic Party, and preached a shrill patriotism exemplified by the ludicrous slogan, "Communism is Twentieth-Century Americanism." ¶ U.S. Congressman **Martin Dies** (1900–1972) was appointed chair of the House Un-American Activities Committee (HUAC) in 1938. Known as the "Dies Committee," it specialized in "investigating" (*i.e.*, persecuting) Left and labor organizations.

WELCOME TO SKID ROAD

In every large city in the United States is a thoroughfare known as the Skid Road. It is so named because it's the habitat of the floating population. In the logging industry the Skid Road is a trough used to skid logs down to the pond for the run down to the mill. With the natural aptness of single men whose only outlook is their mode of livelihood, they named the street in town where they congregate, the Skid Road.

These are men without homes, without women, without votes, without any standing or protection in the community. They are the prey of every vice, charlatan and politician that such a street will breed.

This is the street of a hundred thousand homeless men. Very likely you think they are all panhandlers. But stop and think a moment: Can any city support a hundred thousand panhandlers? Some of them *must* work. As a matter of fact, about seventy-five percent of them are employed, most of them on temporary jobs. A great many of them are just in from the outlands where they have been building dams or roads, or logging or harvesting or farming.

They are an improvident lot, so it won't be long till they are broke and shipping out again. The gambling halls and honky-tonks will get their money and they will be gone again to do the world's work.

Here on this murky, turbulent thoroughfare will be found gandy-dancers and pearl-divers, dingbats and dinoes, muckers and moochers, mule-skinners and mushfakirs, harvest-hands and handymen, tree-fallers and tie-tampers, tinkers and tinhorns, seamen and sandhogs, bindlestiffs and buckers, cokeheads and crumbs, farmers and fruit-tramps, hustlers and highclimbers, jackrollers and jungle-buzzards, pitchmen and plingers, roustabouts and riggers, stewbums and spielers, teamies and tramp-cooks, loggers and linemen, Wobblies and Weary Willies.

This is the Skid Road—home of the submerged tenth, habitat of the homeless and hopeless, street of broken dreams, last ditch of the lost and lonely.

CHICAGO'S HOBO COLLEGES
A Short History

JUST WHEN OR WHERE the first Hobo College was founded I am unable to determine. James Eads How, the "Millionaire Hobo," started several Hobo Colleges in the United States in the first decade of the twentieth century, including one in Chicago which opened around 1907. Strangely, there is nothing about him in any volume of *Who's Who* or other biographical dictionaries. But a few old-timers who are still around remember that he established these colleges "for the continued education of the migratory workers."

A lot of people might object to the term *college* for the open forums they really were. Webster would agree with How, I think: "A society of scholars incorporated for study or instruction." That is at least one of the things we came to these places for. If we had merely wanted to get out of the cold, we could have gone to a mission.

Hobo Colleges were run on the same format as the numerous other open forums around Chicago before the Great Depression. An expert was given up to an hour to expound his pet monomania. After that, we other monomaniacs would spend the rest of the evening showing him the error of his ways. Back around 1914 the great archaeologist James Breasted gave a talk at the Hobo College. Some sheepherder hobo from Montana took issue with his remarks. To prove him wrong he quoted from paragraph five, page gimmel, chapter thirteen of volume two of the works of James Breasted. All during the tirade, the great Egyptologist stood humbly with bowed head, then thanked the scholar from Montana for reproving him.

Another bum tried to get Jane Addams straightened out when she spoke at the Hobo College here. He said her Hull House was just a mustard plaster on the cancer of poverty that was afflicting the nation. All she did was laugh.

Clarence Darrow told how a law student came racing down the corridor of the courthouse to tell him he'd finally passed the bar exams. He told the jubilant student, "Now that you're in you'll want to raise the professional standards."

"Yeah," one of the 'boes told Darrow, "They ain't no different from the stiffs. Once they get in the union they want to build a fence around the job so they can keep everybody else out."

My first visit to the Hobo College was in 1923 or '24. It was run by Dave Tullman somewhere in the ten hundred block on Washington Boulevard. Dave Tullman has been a friend of mine for well over thirty years. He was deported a while back for being a Commie. (He joined the Communist Party in 1933; it took him three months to find out there wasn't any gravy on the Commie train, so he quit.) Dave was American to his fingertips, even if he was born in England. He was smart, tough, aggressive and unscrupulous. The only un-American thing about Dave was his aversion to honest labor. This he would do anything to avoid. He even got married.

As at most Hobo Colleges, the main topics of discussion were religion, economics, and power. To put it another way, we hoboes were out to kill Christ, cops and the boss. On that first visit of mine, Kill-Christ Wilson was the evening's speaker. He told the story of Ebenezer Jones who made a lot of moolah and went to Rome to get the Pope's blessing. He came away from the audience not only with the blessing of His Holiness, but with the gift of a rosary besides. But the great ship *Titanic* sank on the return voyage. "Down went Ebenezer Jones, beads, blessing, and all."

It was at that same College that I first heard Dr Ben Reitman give a talk. A couple of years later, he opened his own College at Desplaines and Washington. It held two hundred people and was usually full of stiffs. It was seldom that there wasn't also a goodly sprinkling of divinity students there, from the Chicago Theological Seminary. My guess is that these kids were getting experience they would never get anywhere else. In those days, where else would any of the clergy come upon open hostility to the church?

Having been nothing but a circus tramp, Ben Reitman was a poor excuse for a Hobo. Many people questioned his competence as a doctor also. But there was one thing Ben was truly great at, and that was pitching. He used to pitch Emma Goldman's books after she had finished speaking to a packed house. His contemporary pitchmen said no one could beat him.

How many organizations Ben had supporting his College I don't know. But I recall many a morning when I went to work without breakfast. As he had done with the rest of the stiffs, he had shaken me down for everything but carfare when he passed the hat.

There was a rumor among the stiffs that Ben had discovered an obscure Foundation that promoted the conversion of Jews to Christianity. It was supposed to have been established about the time of the Revolution, and ever since then had been accumulating gelt that was now ripe for the plucking. How true any of this was I never did learn. But Ben had been converted a short time before, and anyone who knew him would tell you he was very adroit at latching onto any loose shekels lying around.

However, if this Foundation subsidized Ben's College venture, they surely didn't stipulate any restrictions. Those stiffs spent more time on the platform killing Jesus than anything else. Perhaps that was on purpose; it sure gave those future missionaries some experience in handling the antagonistic heathen.

I remember one of them saying to me that Martha Biegler was one of the most bigoted people he had ever met. Somehow I had always associated that word with a religious person, but I had to admit she was all of that. Martha was a bitter atheist and an opponent of everything religious. We laughed at her communism but I'm afraid we bought her anti-religion.

My own theory is that we fulminated against that which oppressed us. Too many children had been forced to listen to the preacher drone on every Sunday morning. Too many of us had grown sick of the threat of eternal hellfire. Beaten people are apt to be bitter about the things that oppress them.

Of all the Hobo Colleges in Chicago, Jack Macbeth's was the greatest. It opened in 1931 at 1118 West Madison Street. There was probably more intellectual talent in that dingy, stinky hall than in any open forum Chicago ever had.

I remember one woman telling me how educated all the guys were at Mac's College. Knowing that most of them were as illiterate as myself, I asked her how she had come to that conclusion. She said, Oh, because Jack Macbeth read and wrote Greek, the Bulgarian General knew more about tactics than Blackjack Pershing, the Cosmic Kid could give you a rundown on any philosopher, and Schultz could always holler, "Von fool at a time."

These were just a few of the brain battery who would show any speaker, on any subject, how wrong he was. They proved him wrong whether he was talking about Cosmic Rays or Shakespeare. Nor did they have to know anything at all about the subject. As the poet Tom Gannon used to say, if they knew what they were talking about, it would make them self-conscious.

Of course, some of them really were knowledgeable. Sam Ball, a union printer, was the greatest teacher I have ever met, although he never got beyond the eighth grade. His best lecture was on the revolutionary leader, Jean-Paul Marat. In thirty-five minutes he would take him from the day he was born to the minute of his death. And we learned French history in the process.

Tom Gannon, an old Wobbly, was another friend from Hobo College days. A few short months after Hitler came to power, he started the *Anti-Nazi Magazine*. He already had pictures from Germany, of Rabbis being beaten by stormtroopers. Articles were submitted free and there was no advertising.

One day the power structure, in the form of Chicago's Red Squad, came around to see if there were any Commies holed up in Mac's College. Downstairs was a blackboard which read, "Tonight: Bruno, Gallileo, Copernicus." One of the cops wanted to know, "Who's this guy Bruno Gallileo Copernicus?"

Mac answered, "He was the first to study the nearer side of the sidereal."

The cops then wanted to know if there were any anarchists around. Trying to needle them further, Mac replied, "No, we throw only verbal bombs."

Thornton Wilder once addressed the Hobo College on "The Purpose of Writing." Commander Seeley showed us how the U.S. Navy protected our foreign exploiters. The Senator from Milwaukee (a pseudonym) instructed us not to put the ding on Clarence Darrow, on account of he was too smart. Professor Charles Heenan of DePaul claimed Kit Marlowe wrote Shakespeare's plays, but Francis Bacon was the choice of Professor Carl Steiner. Mac had to keep these two apart to prevent mayhem.

Carl Shiele would tear up whole packs of playing cards at one time, when he wasn't busy being the anthropological expert. David Rockefeller came from the University of Chicago to learn economics from the real experts, the 'boes. Gale Sullivan talked on drama and literature before he became Assistant Postmaster-General.

Willie Wines explained to us why the law of entail never operated too well in the U.S. He became one of the most respected members of the Illinois bar. Yet not long ago he put finis to that chapter. Like Richard Corey he went to the office "and put a bullet through his head."

My own part in this milieu was rather meager. I took over my first forum in 1932. It was called the Hobo Forum and I think the number was 937 Rush Street. It folded in a few weeks. A year later I made my first attempt to start a College of Complexes at 1317 North Clark Street. I invested all of forty dollars in the joint, but it lasted only three months.

When Jack Macbeth tried to become respectable he moved to the Near North Side and changed the name of his place to the Social Science Institute. In 1936 I opened a new Hobo College in his old place at 1118 West Madison. We named it The Knowledge Box, but most people just went on calling it the Hobo College. A few of the characters from Mac's old place—Deacon Budman, Statistical Slim and Porkchops Shorty—refused to leave their house and home on Skid Road, so I inherited them.

The Knowledge Box declared itself "An Educational Forum Where the Unattached, the Homeless, the Hungry, the Rebel, the Maladjusted and Misfit May Endeavor to Find a Better Way of Life and a Useful Niche in the World." We had lectures every evening and on Sunday at 3 p.m. In February 1937 the *New York Times* ran an Associated Press article about us, "Hobo College Sends SOS for Rent Money." Here's how it described the place:

> The Knowledge Box—decorated with murals (alumni art) of Karl Marx, Mark Twain, Ingersoll, Darwin and others—holds seminars, clinics and forums "every night at 8 sharp." The lecturers next week include a Presbyterian minister, a surgeon, a former alderman, a retired attorney, a dentist, a physical culturist, and a former law partner of Clarence Darrow.

I was the Director and Axel W. Dragstedt was Treasurer. Axel and I used to have a lot of fun baiting the Communist

Party's capitalist-killers. We used to tell them it was a mistake to destroy the capitalists. What *we* wanted was the abolition of the working class. We'd explain that there was no pleasing the working class anyway. When workers are working, they complain about being overworked. When they are unemployed, they complain about not having any work. Needless to say we weren't very popular with these folks.

At that time Nels Anderson was writing a book for the University of Chicago Press. He had already published *The Hobo* in 1923, with one of Axel's poems in it. Yet I heard him on the floor of Reitman's College refer to Axel's "bad poetry." Maybe it was. But Axel had something to say, and he said it cogently with humor. Here is a sample, which is all Tom Gannon can remember of Axel's "Talk With God":

> *Last veek ven full of bible dope in mind I took a valk*
> *Unto the place vere heffin iss and had with Gott a talk.*
> *Vile in dis talk Gott said to me,*
> *"My poy, I'm proud of you,*
> *For I can see you understand vat Yesus tried to do."*

Great or small, most writers prostitute themselves to writing the things their audience will accept. As a consequence much of the alleged great writing of the world is only the reflection of what is acceptable to the people of that time and place. Along with most of the other Hobo writers, Axel never got published because he didn't say the things most people wanted to hear. But we laughed at his comic verse when he recited it in his broken English.

Axel's poems rhymed and had some wry humor. They were not as good as T-Bone Slim's, though. Every time I think of T-Bone's "Lumberjack's Prayer" I gotta laugh:

> *Observe me on my bended legs,*
> *I'm asking you for Ham and Eggs,*
> *And if thou have'st custard pies,*
> *I like, dear Lord, the largest size.*

But I didn't really know T-Bone Slim. I met him only once, when I was walking with Axel on Wells Street. That was 1924. I remember how he was dressed. He wore a highroller hat like I hadn't seen since I left the Seattle Skid Road. I can even remember how he walked. I can't describe it, but only loggers who are used to wearing calked boots that weigh about three pounds apiece walk like that when they are wearing dress shoes. With every step you expect to lift those three pounds, and then your foot seems too light.

After introductions, T-Bone Slim told us about the poem he was working on. It was about Snus (snuff). Naturally I appreciated it, but I've never seen it in print.

The Knowledge Box lasted two winters. Our biggest stunt was a debate with the University of Chicago. There were so many people there I was afraid the floor would cave in. The Knowledge Box team—Statistical Slim, Deacon Budman and Jimmie Rohn—debated the U of C team. By public acclaim, the University team won—but only by a small margin, however. And *we* collected twenty-seven dollars and fourteen cents!

Unfortunately, this last incarnation of the old Hobo College also rode the rails into bankruptcy—in 1937—and Chicago was deprived of its finest institution of higher learning. I didn't manage to recoup my misfortunes until 1951, and then I opened the College of Complexes.

Born of wealthy parents, **James Eads How** (1874–1930) studied at Harvard and Oxford and became a Fabian socialist. Increasingly eccentric during his young manhood, he renounced his wealth and came to relish what he regarded as his messianic role as savior of America's hoboes. His International Brotherhood Welfare Association, often mistakenly identified as a union, was strictly devoted to the spreading of How's reformist ideas, and remained under his tight control. ¶ **Martha Allwina Biegler** was "the most known and highly respected woman" speaker among the Bughouse Square regulars, according to Frank O. Beck (see Bibliography). Born in 1864, she graduated from the University of Indiana, learned typesetting, and worked at the *Chicago Daily Socialist* in 1912. Her legendary rooming house was known to hoboes from coast to coast. A frequenter of the Dil Pickle, she also ran the lively Woman's Forum. The "Where to Go" column in the April 5, 1919 issue of *The New Majority* (a weekly published by the Chicago Federation of Labor) announced a forthcoming meeting at which "the following members of the Woman's Forum—Mabel Kanka, Lucy Parsons, Martha Biegler and Edna Fine—will prove the majority of men are low-grade morons." Biegler died in the late 1930s, not long after her companion, Harry Batters, a street-peddler of Left literature known as "The Ambassador from Moscow." ¶ Born Matt Valentine Huhta in Ashtabula, Ohio, **T-Bone Slim** (*c.* 1880–1942) became one of the IWW's most popular humorists and songwriters—indeed, the union's foremost "Man of Letters." Much of his best work is collected in *Juice Is Stranger Than Friction* (Rosemont, ed., 1992—see Bibliography).

A NIGHT AT THE KNOWLEDGE BOX

Editor's Note: *This excerpt from a play, "Skid Road," is evidently a record of one evening's post-lecture discussions from the floor at Slim Brundage's forum, The Knowledge Box, often simply called the Hobo College.*

DIRECTOR: Gentlemen, it's not every day that we get a full-fledged Professor of Economics to lecture us. I suggest that we give him a vote of thanks. *(Uproarious applause.)* And now that we have got that out of the way, Professor, we will proceed with your education. You thought you came down here to teach us something. Not so, my dear sir. We got you down here to teach *you* something. If you don't believe it, just sit and listen. How many want to educate the Professor? *(Four hands are raised.)* Who wants to be first? As usual, nobody wants to be first. Doctor Lamb, how about you?

Doctor Lamb: I asked the speaker, "What is wealth?" Like every other professor he betrayed his ignorance of the subject. No more understanding of the matter than a baby not yet born. What did Henry George say? What did he say? "Take the tax off industry and put it on the land." And that is the only way we're going to solve the economic problems of the world. Henry Ford has a plan for putting the farmer to work growing automobiles in his cornfields. He has no more understanding than the Professor. If we had a Single Tax it wouldn't be necessary to grow automobiles on a farm.

Director: Thank you very much, Dr Lamb. I'm sure you've given the Professor something to think about. Mr Sheridan, do you want to talk now?

Jimmy Sheridan: The hypothesis which the learned doctor so grandiloquently promulgated finds a response in the nether regions of my medulla oblongata. His esoteric cogitations bespeak a profundity of intellect seldom equaled since Immanuel Kant expostulated the categorical infinitives. However, I must eschew his contention that the conventional concepts of John Dewey antagonize the mathematical precepts expounded by Adam Smith and Karl Marx. Nevertheless, his expiations have intelligibility, veracity and vivacity, which are remarkably free from rodomontade and sonorous bombast. His philosophical and psychological observations possess clarified conciseness, compacted comprehensibility, coalescent consistency and concatenated cogency. Thank you, one and all, for your kind attention.

Director: Thank you, Mr Sheridan, for stopping when you did. A little more of that and we'd have had to get a gas mask. Now you see, Professor, your education is just beginning. You understand by now that, no matter what you said, you're wrong. Next!

Statistical Slim: Just for a change, I think I'll talk on the subject. As I understand it, the subject is, "The Works Progress Administration as a Permanent Institution." As a member of the leisure class, I have viewed the rise of the W.P.A. with intense satisfaction. Like a considerable number of gentry who live by the sweat of another man's brow, the loss of jobs on the part of a great number of people created a crisis, a critical situation, in my life.

Socrates is reputed to have said that the slavery of the many was necessary for the culture of a few. Jobs for the many are necessary for the leisure of us few. What with the drying up of the fountains of generosity on the part of the average and unaverage citizen, and the increase in the number of state and federal relief agencies, it has become a rather taxing problem— not only for the government, but also for the hobo.

We, of the ragged individualist persuasion, are, I'm afraid, faced with the certainty of extinction. In the face of this dire and distressing situation, the W.P.A. stands out on the part of the government to save from the mire of the Depression a struggling and destitute people. Jobs were created and wages rose. Dividends and bond interest soared. We of the leisure class again faced the future with optimism, in expectation of another golden harvest and enjoyment of the leisure and wealth our government struggled so ardently to win for us.

But alas, while one part of our class seems to have been saved from extinction, yet to my sorrow I am afraid to confess that the other part, with its habitat on Skid Road, is irrevocably doomed. For the W.P.A. has converted from the ways of the road a larger and larger number of Weary Willies. Instead of ragged individualists, we hoboes are turning into stylishly dressed citizens with only one vote.

Director: Next.

Deacon Budman: As Deacon of the Knowledge Box and Bughouse Square, I have been asked to give my opinion on this W.P.A. situation. First of all I want to say that my opinion is largely theoretical, because long ago I found that I couldn't make a living working. The boss and I always disagreed. He wanted long hours for short pay, and I wanted long pay for short hours.

This is not the first panic I've been through. In fact, it has been forty-two years of continuous panic and depression. Naturally I've had time to observe, and especially to observe the denizens of the Skid Road.

This is the first time in my forty-two years of unemployment that I have found the government paying a premium on it. In other words, some of the best mission stiffs that have been continuously unemployed have become the aristocrats of the Skid Road.

The time has arrived when it is not considered good form not to have a case-worker. In fact, that dignitary has become a person of great importance on the Skid Road. The time of the depression stiff is taken up with pinochle-playing and trying to figure out how to chisel the case-worker out of a new pair of shoes, or a coat and vest.

As Deacon of the Knowledge Box and Bughouse Square, I want to somewhat disagree with the last speaker. It's not the real hobo who is being eliminated by the W.P.A., but rather the depression stiff, who was created in the slump of 1929.

There was a time when the unemployed was considered an outcast, but now the government places a premium on unemployment, and a penalty for trying to stay off relief.

One congressman wants to pay the unemployed two hundred dollars a month for being unemployed, with the understanding that he must spend it all. I figured it out and found that it came to three dollars a day for meals, and two-fifty for beds. With meals fifteen cents and beds twenty-five cents, that would be ten beds and twenty-five meals a day. That would be too much like work.

Director: It seems to me that you fellows are trying to talk on the subject, but it's a question whether you are or not—sort of an is-and-is-not affair. Reminds me of my friend, Attorney Wines, when he was talking on Platonic love. He said that he liked the idea, but his lady friends were always spoiling it by getting pregnant. Next!

Porkchops Shorty: As a hobo of long travels and short lunches, I have been asked to give my opinion of the W.P.A. I feel flattened—I mean flattered by this offer to bring before this audience these ideas of mine. The opportunity to present the ideas of so large and uninfluential a body of men as the American hobo does not occur every day.

It may perhaps be of interest to you in the audience to know how it happens that such a well-known orator and such an eloquent speaker as myself should happen to be among the ranks of men so little known.

Now it can be told. The reason I am a hobo lays in my unfortunate heredity. You see, work holds a deadly terror for me, because of family reasons. My brother died going to work. My sister died coming *from* work. My old man died *at* work. And I may die from *lack* of work. You can see that, with a family history such as this, I cannot in all fairness approach the subject of work with an unbiased attitude.

The very name *work* in the Works Progress Administration leaves me with a feeling of horror. I think the W.P.A. would be a good thing if it didn't have that word *work* in it. Now if it was changed to Pleasure Progress Administration, or Plate of Porkchops Administration, I could feed easier—I mean *feel* easier.

I consider the W.P.A. a Progressive Works Administration—a boon to those that want work, and a godsend to those that won't work, for those that won't work must live from those that will.

A printer by trade, **Henry George** (1839–1897) became well known as an economist, social critic and promoter of the Single Tax—the notion that the entire tax burden should be laid on land. He defended his theories in many books, most notably *Progress and Poverty* (1877–79).

NINA SPIES

Editor's note: *Nina van Zandt, daughter and heiress of the chief chemist of the James Kirk soap company, graduated from Vassar in 1883. Like many "society ladies," she decided—just for amusement—to attend a session of the 1886 "Chicago Anarchist Trial." Initially prejudiced against the defendants, her observation of the trial quickly changed her mind. "I soon found that the officers of the court and the entire police and detective force were bent upon the conviction of these men—not because of any crime of theirs, but because of their connection with the labor movement. Animated by a feeling of horror produced by what I saw and heard, and no less by a feeling of justice, I determined to range myself on the side of the persecuted."*

An interview with defendant August Spies, editor of the anarchist daily Arbeiter-Zeitung, *resulted in a mutual "feeling of amity" which rapidly evolved into "a strong affection." Not long afterward, Nina van Zandt became the wife of one of the foremost political prisoners in the U.S. But on November 11, 1887, young Mrs Spies became a widow, for her husband and three of his comrades were put to death by the State of Illinois for the crime of defending the rights of labor.*

Ostracized in the press and cut off from her inheritance, Nina Spies remained active in the radical workers' movement up to her death in 1937. She was especially close to the IWW and the Hobo Colleges. Her rooming house was home to many hoboes as well as a large number of stray cats and dogs.

WEST MADISON STREET: Street without sorrows, without happiness, without laughter or tears. "Stupid and stunned, brother to the ox." Such are the denizens of this thoroughfare of a hundred thousand homeless men.

A few paces to the left, Nina hobbled along on her poor old rheumatic feet. Two well-dressed punks came out of a two-bit flophouse. As they passed I heard one say, "See that old lady? She eats food out of garbage cans."

Time was when the news headlines of the world blared Nina's name. But these punks didn't know that. How could they? That was forty years ago. How could they, with their petty visions, know that the fires of life had seared the soul of this woman? That the dross had been burned away, leaving the pure alloy?

Forty years ago, when Nina had just left college (in those days a college degree meant something), she was a fine figure of a woman. All the vistas of life opened before her. Perhaps she was then as contemptuous as those punks are now.

Then came the Haymarket Massacre, where the cops marched in Chicago's Haymarket Square to stop the Free Speech. That was in 1886. The speakers were fighting for the eight-hour day.

August Spies was connected with the anarchist group. Now he was in jail, falsely charged with murder. After a frame-up trial, he and his fellow workers were convicted. There were rumors of a new trial. Or perhaps the governor might pardon the anarchists? But no, they must hang.

One must go where the heart leads. A futile gesture, perhaps, but Nina Van Zandt became Mrs August Spies—married by proxy in the death cell.

The small-souled are embittered by adversity, but the great hearts are only strengthened by it. As the fire burns out the dross and leaves the pure steel, so did the tragedy of August Spies' judicial murder by the State of Illinois fill Nina's heart with compassion for every living thing.

Man, woman, child, cat or dog—any who were in need could share all that was Nina's, to the last crust. Now she is old and broken and crippled. And two punks can say they saw her rooting in garbage cans.

Sure she was—rooting in garbage cans to feed a bunch of stray cats and dogs that the rest of the world is too busy with their own petty affairs to worry about.

Will you and I, when we are old and crippled, so that every step is misery, still have enough bigness of heart to bother with the less fortunate creatures?

STATISTICAL SLIM
Laziness With Ability

H IS NAME IS Statistical Slim and he may be found any night between eleven and one at the Penny Cafeteria on Madison and Halsted Streets in Chicago. This Penny Cafeteria is a fitting place for Slim. It serves the world's worst food at the world's lowest price. For Slim is the most classic description of the word *bum* that one may find the world over.

To those who are unacquainted with the submerged tenth, let it be said that bum is a particular brand of the genus *stiff*. There are hoboes, tramps, bums and many other subdivisions such as stewbums, circus tramps and harvest 'boes.

But Slim is just plain bum. A hobo is a migratory worker. A tramp is a migratory nonworker. And a bum is a nonmigratory nonworker. That's Slim. He's so lazy he won't wash his neck.

Two things set Slim apart from the rest of the world: his laziness, which is proverbial even on the Skid Road, where none of us is very ambitious, and his ability to think. There are more brains on the Stem than one would suspect.

Last winter Slim was the custodian of our Hobo College. Swell atmosphere. He would arise in soleless shoes and unshaven face, and deliver a lecture on "The Ineffability of the Whichness and Whereas." It sure knocked the slummers for a loop. All of them would look at him and say, "The poor fellow, such a mind. If only he had a chance!"

One lady said she wished she had money to dress Slim up and get a few porkchops under his ribs, and see what the result would be. But Statistical Slim had been dressed up before—all to no effect. Two days after being dressed up he was the same old bum.

What's wrong with this guy? Don't tell me he ain't got all his marbles. We know that. And even so, he's got more on the ball than a lot of bigshots I know.

Usually when we meet up with ability it doesn't take long to discover why the bird who's got it isn't in the dough. Sometimes it's because the guy is too smart and tries to take on everybody. More often it's weakness, like wine or women. But with Slim it's just plain laziness.

But laziness is an ambiguous term. It may mean anything. More often than not there is a physical or psychical reason for it. Ordinarily it's the lack of guts. In this society, most people haven't got what it takes to get a job done without a master standing over them with a whip. If it wasn't for the time-clock the world's work would never get done.

Slim has so much of that old American individualism that he can't stand the whip of a steady job. To say that he hasn't guts enough to be his own master is not true. But then, maybe it is. I don't know. I do know that he's got plenty of the old fortitude.

An occasion arose one time where I thought Statistical Slim had gone south with a fan that belonged to me. Hunting him up, I demanded an explanation. Slim rose up on his hind legs like an angry gamecock ready to do battle. He stated in no uncertain terms that he didn't take my blankety-blank electric fan, and what was more, he played the game straight—and so forth and so on. And if I didn't like it I could do what I blankety-blank pleased about it.

Now of course I'm no tough guy. But then, I ain't been taken to the cleaners in some time. And it's a long time since porkchops and me were strangers. The same can't be said of Statistical Slim. He misses more meals than he gets. He knows these things. He knows that if it comes to battle he's probably due for a tamping. But he's got guts enough to stand up and take it.

Maybe there are different types of guts. Maybe a guy can have one kind of courage and not another. But it does seem to me that a man who's got what it takes to take a tamping ought to have what it takes to get some of the things that he wants from life.

But then, maybe he doesn't really want three meals a day. Or a decent shirt on his back. After all, most of us strive to get the things from life we want most. What in hell does Statistical Slim want?

One thing he wants is that everybody should say his word is as good as his bond. Evidently that's more important to him than a clean shirt.

Aw hell, you figure it out.

THE COSMIC KID
IN KANGAROO COURT

Editor's note: Bughouse Square and the Hobo Colleges were enlivened by many outstanding hobo thinkers. Few were stranger or more brilliant than English-born Herbert William Shaw, better known as the Cosmic Kid. Jack Sheridan described him as "the first soapboxer to take his audience on philosophic flights into empyrean realms of thought." Journalist George Murray, who also knew him in Dil Pickle days, recalled that Shaw "thought of philosophy as an unending quest. He believed that when a man resolves life into certainties, he is finished as an investigator. Thus the acceptance of any philosophical formula— in the field of religion or politics or economics—meant the death of the philosopher as such" (see Bibliography).

The following sketch is excerpted from a draft of a play, "Kangaroo Court," in which several other distinguished hobo philosophers also make their appearance.

The Cosmic Kid died in his seventies in the mid-1950s. Jack Sheridan delivered his eulogy in a special ceremony in Bughouse Square.

CLERK OF COURT: The Hoboes of the Knowledge Box *versus* the Cosmic Kid, charged with Violation 1118 of the educational statutes of the State of Knowledge, to wit: maliciously and perversely, premediated and with knowledge aforethought, conspiring with the aid of the dictionary, abetted by ignorance, to confuse, abuse and otherwise misuse the English language by harranguing in a loud and discreditable manner, mixing up synonyms, abusing adjectives, distorting pronouns and using long and weighty words on light subjects, thereby hiding from view the true meaning of his thoughts (if he has any) and thereby driving many poor and defenseless citizens to despair, rage and otherwise provocating anger, endangering the peace, comfort and health of the community.

Judge, to defendant: Did you do all *that*?

Cosmic Kid: By the sacred hoof of my hybrid aunt in Angor I would not be guilty of such a malefaction, Your Orneryness.

Judge: You plead Not Guilty then?

Cosmic Kid: So long as my respiratory organs function with the least degree of normalcy, I shall plead for my organic and hereditary constitutionality.

Chorus of lawyers: Let me defend you. . . I'll get you off. . . Try me this once.

Cosmic Kid: Shall I, who have transported the eagle of England o'er the seven seas, be insulted by having vultures such as present themselves here defend me before such an inconsequential tribunal?

Judge: What's he talking about, 'Cutor?

Prosecutor: Your guess is as good as mine, judge. I reckon he wants to defend himself.

The Dil Pickle Club in Tooker Alley (woodcut, 1920s)

Ben Reitman

A RUN-IN WITH BEN REITMAN

Editor's note: *Among Chicagoans with hobo connections, the best known was undoubtedly Dr Ben Reitman (1879–1942), a physician specializing in venereal diseases who operated what Slim Brundage elsewhere in these pages calls the city's "most successful Hobo College." Although the renowned "clap doctor" and the future Janitor of the College of Complexes must have run into each almost daily over a period of nearly twenty years, little is known of their association. The following anecdote suggests that they did not regard each other with high esteem.*

Roger A. Bruns has written a sympathetic, full-length biography of Reitman, who is also mentioned in numerous memoirs (see Bibliography).

BEN REITMAN always got a big bang out of shocking the unwary. One time he brought thirty-five divinity students into a saloon where I was tending bar. "Now, Slim," he boomed in his pitchman's voice, "tell these people how you justify yourself."

I said, "I don't know what you're talking about. Why should I justify anything?"

"You claim you want to see a better world. How can you justify selling booze, if that is so?"

"Huh!" I said, "why should I justify it? I'm selling people something they want. If no one wanted to buy religion, these students wouldn't be going into the business of selling it. If no one wanted hooch, I wouldn't be selling it."

Then the big mountebank came on with his punchline. "You see, young people, Slim wants a world without booze, but the time is not ripe. So he's a bartender. I want to see a world without venereal disease, but the time is not yet. So I make a living being a clap doctor."

But it's a lie. I don't ever want to see a world without *spiritus fermenti*. Just as soon as I find somebody who hasn't any better sense than to invest in me, I'm going back in the saloon business.

AXEL DRAGSTEDT
Poet Laureate of West Madison Street

Editor's note: In The Hobo *(1923), Nels Anderson called Swedish-born Axel W. Dragstedt "a prominent personality in Chicago's Hobohemia," and devoted a page and a half to him as an example of "The Hobo Intellectual."*

In the text published here, the Janitor recalls Anderson as an unfriendly critic of Dragstedt's verse. In The Hobo, *however, Anderson cites him as "a poet of no mean ability."*

The College of Complexes Archives includes a substantial file of Dragstedt's correspondence.

AXEL DRAGSTEDT is my oldest friend. Back in the old days of the Hobo College, when most of you punks were no more than a lascivious leer in the old man's eye, Axel and I were kidding the pants off the Communists, who wanted to kill the capitalists. We sponsored a move to abolish the working class instead. And when the good trade unionists started featherbedding to protect themselves against machines, we hollered for bigger and better machines. We said, "Let the machines do all the work!" We were perfectly willing to sit in the shade and watch the machines do it.

Of course these were gags. But now the United States is frightened by these very things: the liquidation of the working class, and automation—if you believe Secretary of Labor Wirtz and others.

By that time Axel was forty-five and had retired from his job of moving pianos. Long before that he had been foreman of a section gang, building railroads. His last job was messenger for Western Union.

Nels Anderson once said that Axel wrote bad poetry, but we boys in the Hobo College got a bang out of it. The other artists at Chicago's first street art fair said his figurines stunk, but he sold more than anyone else. The King of the Soapboxers said Axel was crazy, but he sure came up with some original thinking now and then.

In 1955 he retired to Hot Springs, Arkansas, to become a philosopher. His latest opus is *1960, or, Why People Do What*

They Do. Here are some quotes:

> *Our rulers are hell-bent to have us turned into the world's greatest cannon-fodder factory.*

> *Not one in a million has any idea of living except to pay officials and give them the power to make us obey them—which is the same as telling the most vicious nut in the insane asylum, "I will pay whatever you want if you will force me to do whatever you want me to do."*

> *People who pay office-holders to make their final decisions can have only what the office-holders want.*

> *We do not only expect someone else to do our thinking for us, but eagerly await our rulers' orders to lie, steal and kill.*

Axel's answer to the damned foolishness of this state of affairs is what he calls the collective way of life. It is the same principle as the old Roman forum. All final decisions will be made by the people in meetings assembled. Right away all the so-called "wise" characters are going to squawk that this society is too big and involved for such a cumbersome form of self-government. Bull-oney, says Axel—that is just an organizational problem. If it can be done small, it can be done big.

Last week in *U.S. News and World Report*, a former bigshot in the United Nations beefs that the "free world" is losing out to the Commies, because "we" are doing all the wrong things. Why didn't they just ask Axel? He was telling them the same thing twenty years ago. Of course, he's just a "dumb Swede." And he don't play with the powers that be.

MEMOIRS OF A DIL PICKLER
FIFTY YEARS OF FREE-SPEECH FORUMS IN CHICAGO

OVER THIRTY-FIVE YEARS ago I was sitting in Bughouse Square with a tramp reporter named Red Terry, who hailed from New York's Greenwich Village. We got to talking about Chicago's Dil Pickle Club—the predecessor of the College of Complexes.

Red contended that the Dil Pickle was absolutely unique, that there was nothing like it in the whole world, that it was the intellectual center of America, and that it never could have happened anywhere else but in Chicago.

"Believe me," he said, "I know. I was raised in Greenwich Village and I've made the scene in every hobohemia across the country."

This surprised me because I thought Greenwich Village was America's intellectual center. Red argued that it was only the artistic center; when people went to the Village, he said, they went looking for poets, writers, artists, and other longhaired members of the Great Unwashed. But when they came to Chicago's Near North Side, they were looking for the bums who talked like college professors.

Then I remembered that was how I originally found the place. A dentist dragged me there one day, little suspecting I was one of the bums (I had a clean shirt on that day).

What was the Dil Pickle Club? One of the Pickle's brighter denizens, whose feet I used to sit at, wrote this poem about the place in 1920:

The Dil Pickle Club
by Bert Weber

'Twas a poor old barn in the Alley,
Dirty and dark and bare.
The home of rats and alley cats.
And nobody seemed to care.

It stood like a tramp deserted

And thousands passed it by,
No one to give it a helping hand,
Just left in the alley to die.

Then came a feller names Jones,
From his eyes the tears did trickle,
He adopted that poor old orphan barn
and christened it The "Dil Pickle."

He gave it the care of a mother,
And nursed it on calcimine.
Cured all the panes in it's windows,
And swabbed it with turpentine.

Till it shown with the bloom of beauty
And bathed in electric light,
It welcomed its friends and victims
In the meetings there at night.

It welcomed it's friends and victims,
The friends and lovers of art.
And fed both the brain and the belly.
La Bohemia, Alley carte.

With music by Rudolph von Liebich,
In his nightshirt trimmed in pink,
And the beautiful rhyme of Bodenheim
To Minna his missing link.

It will save the world's heart from breaking,
Free China from the Jap.
Give home rule to old Ireland,
And the lakefront back to Cap.

Twas a poor old barn in the alley,
But gone is the dire disgrace,
The aristocrat must doff his hat
To that "Pickle" of Tooker Place.

Bert Weber is still living in Twin Lakes, Wisconsin. His most famous poem was the allegedly sacrilegious "Jesus Wept." A couple of his very fine plays were produced a number of times at the Pickle over the years: *The Plagues of Egypt* and *The First Triangle*. Bert was one of the finest writers ever to come in the Dil Pickle door, but he never had any ambition to write professionally.

But what *was* the Pickle? Art center, little theater, indoor Bughouse Square, Bohemian tourist trap, latter-day hangout for country-store Solons, or just a dive for nuts? Maybe it was all of these things. How would I know? I was just one of the habitués. Considering myself a young pseudo-intellectual, it was home to me. Home is where the heart is. Home is where you establish rapport with other humans. Or, if you want to be nasty about it, sub-humans. Who cares?

Most people recall the Dil Pickle Club today because of the famous writers who went there. Long ago such characters as Carl Sandburg, Ben Hecht, Sherwood Anderson and Max Bodenheim moved on to greener pastures, far from Chicago. Since I could write a little myself, I wasn't so impressed by these guys. In any case, they weren't the people most of us came to the Dil Pickle to see—or rather to hear. Since most of us were uneducated workingstiffs, what we wanted was knowledge, learning, a liberal education. So it was the real thinkers of the day who enthralled us, such as philosopher T.V. Smith and the Swedish physiologist, Anton Carlson. At the Pickle, they were packing the house Standing-Room-Only. Such lesser lights as assistant professor Andrew Ivy (later of Krebiozen fame); A. E. Emerson, a world authority on zoology; and the noted surgeon Dr Lester Dragstedt, whom you've probably seen in *Life* magazine, also drew good-sized crowds.

Of course most of us Picklers were fearfully young and insecure. It was understood that none of us would ever amount to anything playing around a joint like that. Weren't we the Great Unwashed? Didn't respectable people warn their teenagers not to hang around with us?

A few of us didn't turn out so badly after all. One young Dil Pickle poet became one of the great lawyers in the state. (I won't mention his name since admitting he knows me might jeopardize his position.) James T. Farrell used to drink bathtub gin out of the same bottle with me. I have five autographed books of his—all in foreign languages, which I guess makes him an international figure. A couple of others in the gang have made a million or five, but that's so mundane they don't even want word about it to get around.

Not all Dil Pickle lecturers were professors, or even great brains. In fact, when business was poor for a few weeks we would surely be treated to a sex lecture. That, we knew, was to pay the rent. Back then you couldn't find sex for sale at every newsstand or movie-house. You had to stumble down a dark alley, kick around some garbage, step high, stoop, squeeze and crawl into a place like the Dil Pickle to catch up on such matters. Even so, the sex lectures didn't draw better than a top name from the University of Chicago like Horatio Hackett Newman or Albert Michelson.

I recall one of Lester Dragstedt's talks in 1924. His cousin Axel and I crawled out of our Skid Road flophouse and walked three miles to the Pickle to heckle him. We had to stand for two hours. Dragstedt was just an assistant then but he was talking about a wonder drug. It seems to me Jack Jones, the owner of the Pickle, billed him as one of the developers of Insulin, but the doctor's son tells me his dad didn't know nothing about anything but surgery.

Elbert Hubbard said that Voltaire was a true philosopher because he could laugh at himself. So could we. My wife was an artist. I was a housepainter. This was typical of the place and the time. I'm not so sure we were any smarter than the other people round and about. It was just that we were forced to think in the climate engendered there. I know we used to get hold of an idea, kick it around, exhaust all the possibilities in it, digest it, spit it out. A couple of years after we had forgotten about it some great brain like H. L. Mencken would spew it forth as an example of his own brilliant thinking.

How did the Dil Pickle Club get started? And how did it get its unusual and oddly-spelled name?

In 1914 a bunch of soapboxers from Bughouse Square began worrying about how they were going to keep the snowballs off themselves through the winter. In those days the

Ozone Orators, as soapboxers were sometimes called, were looked upon with justified respect. When a speaker finished his tirade in the Square, he would step down and pass the hat. Good soapboxers made a fairly decent living at it, and because of this, some of them had enough money to pool their resources that winter to rent a place at the end of Pearson Street to put a roof over their activities. Because he was a poor speaker, Jack Jones was crowned janitor and custodian of the place. Being soapboxers, and therefore much concerned with freedom, and especially freedom from responsibility, the others often forgot to divvy up their share of the rent. But somehow Jones always managed to come up with it. As a result, he wound up sole proprietor, in full possession of the Pickle.

The story of how the Dil Pickle got its name is perhaps apocryphal, but here it is—the way I heard it from Bertie Weber. Jim Larkin, dockworker Union organizer from Dublin, had to take it on the lam from his native shore and landed in Chicago. He was one of the founders of the Pickle. One day he, Jones and the others were standing in the barroom of the old Turner Hall on Clark Street. Larkin, who had never tasted dill pickles in the old country, was eating all he could grab out of Old Man Appel's free lunch. Jim held up a pickle and said, "Here is a noble piece of merchandise. Why don't we call our place the Dill Pickle Club?"

It wasn't long before Jones moved the club from Pearson Street to a site more to his liking, and where it was to gain its greatest repute: 18 Tooker Alley. This was a huge old stable in back of 858 North State Street. All Pickle publicity included instructions on how to get there: "Thru the Hole in the Wall, Down Tooker Alley to the Green Lite Over the Orange Door." The club's famous motto was lettered on the entrance: "Step high, stoop low, leave your dignity outside." This wasn't hard to do—you quite literally had to squeeze through a hole in the wall, stoop low (the door was only about four feet high) and literally crawl to get into the evil-smelling barn.

In this new place Jones dropped one of the L's in Dill— probably because some lawyer told him to. I think they were worried about a trademark infringement, and thought the odd spelling would help them avoid a lawsuit.

Jack had a bad eye through which he squinted up at you, and the middle finger of his left hand was missing. One time I asked him how he lost it. He told me a steamboat ran over it in the Chicago River. But a broken-down housepainter told me he was making a bomb to plow up plate-glass windows and it went off in his hand. You guess. For sure he wasn't much of a bomb-maker. One guy said he could break more windows with a single milk bottle than with any number of Jones's bombs.

What kind of a man was Jack Jones? A woman who used to come to the Dil Pickle called herself a psychic, and she classified people according to mineral types. She described Jones the best. She said he was a calcium type—very hard. That was Jones. A real tough guy. I don't mean pugnacious, just very unbending.

Jones was the entrepreneur of the Pickle. He had a beak like a hawk and a mind like a rat, and a meaner man never walked the bridge of the Bounty. He was an ex-Wob—it seems like all of us were Wobs at one time or another. He was also a lousy housepainter—we were members of the same AFL local. I commented on Jones's terrible paint job in the Dil Pickle, pointing at how the stains were poorly mixed and came out all different colors. "You mean you can make them all be the same color?" he asked me.

He had a big cartoon at the entrance of the Club, a man with his mouth wide open, shouting, "We gotta change the system!" But Jack Jones was serious only about one thing: how to further Jack Jones. If he had to be a capitalist to do it, he'd be a capitalist.

In 1924 and for a number of years thereafter I worked at the Dil Pickle Club. I was the bouncer. This was during Prohibition, so Jones didn't sell any booze in the place. So people used to "bottle up"—take up a collection. Anyone who wanted to drink would pitch in. One night one of the waiters sent me out for some bootleg booze that two guys said they wanted. I brought it back and handed it to them, and they said, "You're under arrest." They were Prohibition agents, and they pinched the joint on that evidence. Of course they couldn't pin anything on Jones, who sold only coffee and sandwiches, so they got me.

I didn't have any money. And of course Jones wouldn't pay my fine. Instead, he banned me from the Dil Pickle Club, since he thought I would make the place "suspicious."

Later there was some fight over a woman, and some guy said he was going to beat the hell out of Jones. I got a message that Jones wanted to see me. Jones says, "There's going to be trouble here, and I need you to support me." I laughed at him. Jones never supported anybody—he sure never supported me when I got arrested at the Dil Pickle Club. I told him I wouldn't support him on anything.

I think that if Jones had stayed out of debt, the Dil Pickle Club might have lasted through the Depression. It was open to anyone with the price of admission, which was always cheap. He always managed to pack the house; there were very popular dances every Saturday night. Jones used to drive around in an orange and black truck painted with a quote from Sherwood Anderson calling the Dil Pickle Club "the Only Bright Spot in Chicago." But in the end he overextended himself. He had five buildings, and the rent just got too big. The Dil Pickle Club folded in 1933.

People are always asking me how the College of Complexes started. "How did you ever think up such an unusual saloon?" All we did at the College was put a bar onto the same kind of operation the Dil Pickle had. And the Pickle really wasn't anything new even when it started. Red Terry maintained that the Dil Pickle was peculiar to Chicago and could not exist anywhere else, but in fact it was not unique in this city. In Chicago, somebody was always starting an intellectual forum. In my time there were The Temple of Wisdom, The Gold Coast House of Correction, The Lower Depths, The Seven Arts, The Oasis, The Montparnasse, The Social Science Institute, The Intellectual Inferno and The Pindarians. And these are only the ones whose names I can remember. There were between thirty and forty other open forums in Chicago in the 1920s and '30s. And in addition to these clubs there were the individual personalities who attracted immense audiences in big public theaters. They lectured on Sunday mornings, probably in opposition to the formal churches. Arthur Morrow Lewis is a name old-timers still recall.

Most of the forums had their brief moment of glory and then vanished from the scene. The Seven Arts and the Montparnasse were among the very few—apart from the Pickle—that lasted more than a year.

The Seven Arts was run by Ed Clasby. He was quite a character, very sharp. And he was pretty much openly gay, which in those days was difficult. Those people took a lot of abuse. Clasby lectured for the College of Complexes, billed as the "most libidinous louse in literature, buccaneer of boudoirs and bombastic biographer of Shaw, Wells and Wilde."

Monte Randall ran the Montparnasse. Monte was a great dresser and he used a lot of big words. A lot of people said there was nothing to him, that he didn't know what he was talking about. But he was an extremely intelligent man, very talented. We used to go to his apartment and pass around the stick—that is, marijuana: we really didn't think of it as a drug in those days. After a while we'd all be feeling good, and Monte would take to the piano and play beautifully until all hours of the morning.

Some of these clubs rented whole buildings, some of them met in restaurant banquet rooms. One was in a garret and several were tea-rooms. Some had artistic pretensions and/or tried to produce plays. In all these places books were spoken of with as much respect as people in Wrigley Field talked about the World Series. But the main thing they all had in common—their reason for existence—was the open forum. And the backbone of all these meetings was provided by the ten thousand or more "forum-hounds," as they were called. I knew forum-hounds who went to their first lecture in a downtown theater at ten o'clock in the morning and kept going all day. In the mid-afternoon they went to the Anthropological Society. Around midnight they might be leaving some place like the Dil Pickle Club. One of these folks told me he had gone to six forums on one Sunday. These free-speech zealots were as assiduous in their attendance at all kinds of forums as firebugs at fires or courtbugs at court. And the habitués of the Bug Club were just called Bugs.

The Bug Club held its meetings outdoors on the grass in Washington Park on Chicago's south side. More formally it was called the Washington Park Forum. As many as three thousand people would be there listening to speakers on a Sunday afternoon. And just a mile north of Chicago's busiest street is Bughouse Square, at Clark and Walton, right in front of Newberry

Library. Listed on maps as Washington Square, it's the city's best known free-speech center, where any night of the week (weather permitting) you could hear soapboxers spouting off about anything and everything under the sun.

If the Dil Pickle was the foul weather and late-evening friend of the soapbox orators, Bughouse Square remained their fair weather battleground. I have to admit, though, that I was never as impressed with the level of speakers at Bughouse Square as I was with those of the Bug Club. I guess by the time I arrived on the scene the real glory days of Bughouse Square, when folks like Gene Debs used to address huge crowds there, were pretty much over. Basically, I agree with the guy who first told me about Bughouse Square, a south side Irishman: "I went up to dat Bughouse Square, and I listened to dem guys for about an hour. You know the problem wid dem guys is, dey're tryin' to t'ink. But dey ain't got nuttin' to t'ink wid!"

I started going to forums from practically the first day I got to Chicago, in 1922. I was a Wobbly, a member of the Industrial Workers of the World. And many Wobblies went to forums.

Today, a lot of the younger generation are in the habit of looking at kooks who inhabit the Bug Club and Bughouse Square as an inferior breed of animal. So did a lot of the squares back in those days, too. The big difference is that there were a lot more "Bugs" around then. I prefer to use the word Bugs instead of the modern kook because that is what we all called ourselves.

The U.S. declared war against Germany in April of 1917. Chicago was considered a hotbed of sedition. Anti-war sentiment was high. Mayor William Hale Thompson, I'm told, was openly pro-German. At some point during the war the city government attempted to close down the Bug Club. Just why the Chicago cops wanted to run all the Bugs out of the park I do not know. Weren't they all just a bunch of harmless nuts who liked the sound of their own voices? That's what the powers that be often said about us, before the war started. But now, for some reason, someone in the city government issued orders to clamp down.

Back in those days, however, there were quite a few characters around who thought free speech was important—even if there was a war on. The attempt to suppress the Bug Club made them so mad that they got a petition up for an injunction against the Chicago police department restraining them from molesting the "Bugs." Some character by the name of Clarence Darrow was the first name on it. Following his moniker were fifteen thousand others. They got the injunction, the police were restrained, and the Bug Club carried on.

In the Bug Club or at Bughouse Square, if anybody had anything to say he just stood up and started yakking. If he said it well he had a tremendous audience. If he was a rank tyro, as I was in those days, he still had a few kindly souls to listen. Sometimes there would be three or four meetings going all at once, with three thousand people getting free entertainment. Besides the big gatherings there were also the "beehives," much smaller meetings—basically just arguments that a few people clustered around to listen to.

I think I was nineteen that year. There was a tall old man, in his eighties, a Catholic, who used to argue religion with me, because I was a very devout atheist in those years. I must have won the argument that day because some lady jumped all over me for "picking on an old man." My only defense was that Murphy had traveled all the way from Niles Center to the Bug Club just to argue religion with somebody. If he didn't like it, why would he spend half a day on the streetcars just to get there?

As a matter of fact we were quite friendly, the old man and I. He used to tell strangers that atheists were good for Catholics, "like fleas on a dog. If a dog didn't have fleas he wouldn't remember he was a dog."

People who had been to England claimed that London's Hyde Park couldn't hold a candle to the Bug Club as an open forum. The quality of the discourse over there, they said, was far below that of the Bugs. Most of the audience in London's Hyde Park were mere curiosity seekers. Our audiences were all Bugs. Very few people just passed by and stopped. We were too well hidden by the trees. If you were there it was because you wanted to be there and because you were interested.

Chicago Magazine once [in 1954] called the College of Complexes "spurious." Nothing burns me up like being called a phony. Years ago they used to accuse us at the Dil Pickle Club of the same thing—of being "phony." True, we proudly wore the badge of "pseudo-intellectual." That meant we *played* at intellectualism. Few of us made our living at it—unless you call copywriting intellectualism. Other people got their exercise pushing a little pill around a field, and we got ours pushing our gray matter against each other's. Perhaps it didn't do anybody any good, but the one thing that made the Dil Pickle survive in the memory of Chicagoans was that it wasn't phony. Jack Jones was called every kind of a blackguard that the facile tongues of the habitués could devise. But because he was a hard-rock miner, and as solid as that rock, we never called him phony. Slimy, but never phony.

How phony were we? I've already mentioned that one of those Dil Pickle pseudo-intellectuals is now the legal brains for one of the greatest states of the union, and another has the reputation of being the world's greatest author. I'm not talking about the Darrows, Hemingways, Sandburgs or Hechts who just came there on occasion, but of the regulars. Among the habitués I can think of a dozen names who are at the top of their professions today.

I dwell upon these gatherings of free-speech-lovers at the Dil Pickle, the Bug Club, Bughouse Square and other open forums because they are as indigenous to Chicago as our thirty-five miles of lakefront, our boulevard system and stockyards.

In his book *The Public Philosophy* Walter Lippman contends that what made American democracy work was free interchange in the marketplace of ideas. He also states that we are losing this democracy because of the lack of that interchange.

What I have been trying to show here is that such interchange was one of the major characteristics of Chicago for many years.

Why was public discussion such a popular sport in this city? And what happened to it?

The answers aren't easy, but here's a few things to think about.

It's no accident that there have been more isms started in Chicago than any other place in America. The first important strike for the eight-hour day took place here. Most of the great radical movements, including the Socialist Party, the Industrial Workers of the World and the Communist Party, started here. So did innumerable labor unions. Most of America's new religions, some of which became worldwide, started here. The *Bulletin of Atomic Scientists* is published here. Slice it any way you want, I call these dynamic intellectual movements.

Nowadays most of the radicals are dead. The labor unions' headquarters have moved to Washington, D.C., and the religions to Los Angeles. Bughouse Square and the Bug Club attract only a handful of listeners. But I think Red Terry was basically right: The Dil Pickle Club and other open forums were unique Chicago institutions. They were fulfilling a need—something the people of Chicago wanted.

Is that something almost gone? Or is it something that may be coming back? Who knows?

We'll just have to see what happens when I get the College of Complexes going again!

The IWW's best-known composer, **Rudolf von Liebich** wrote the music for "We Have Fed You All a Thousand Years" and other Wobbly favorites, and played at Joe Hill's funeral in Waldheim Cemetery in 1915. He was also Musical Director of the Dil Pickle Club. ¶ Remembered today primarily as an outrageous bohemian buffoon, Mississippi-born **Max Bodenheim** (1893–1954) was a poet (*Minna and Myself*, 1918; *Against This Age*, 1925; *Bringing Jazz*, 1930), novelist (*Replenishing Jessica*, 1925), and co-editor (with Ben Hecht) of the *Chicago Literary Times*, 1923–24. For many years a member of the Communist Party, after World War II he frequented the IWW and the Libertarian Socialist League in Chicago. ¶ Dil Pickle Club manager **Jack Archibald Jones** had been an IWW organizer in Minnesota and Montana, and for several years the husband of IWW organizer Elizabeth Gurley Flynn. Jones left the union in 1912 to join William Z. Foster's short-lived Syndicalist League of North America. Something of a crank, he was a militant teetotaler and in his later years devoted much time to technocracy and designing a new calendar. He also invented and manufactured a toy, the Du-Dil-Duck, which some have regarded as a model for a more successful duck drawn by Chicago cartoonist Walt Disney. Jones died in 1940. ¶ A major figure in the Irish labor movement, **James Larkin** (1876–1947) was secretary of the Irish Transport and General Workers' Union, 1909–24, and editor of the *Irish Worker*. In the U.S., 1914–23, he was active in the Left Wing of the Socialist Party around Charles H. Kerr's *International Socialist Review*, and was a featured speaker at Joe Hill's funeral in 1915. A co-founder of the Communist Labor Party in Chicago, 1919, he was indicted for "criminal anarchy" later that year; sentenced to Sing-Sing for five-to-ten years, he was deported to Ireland in 1923. ¶ After the Dil Pickle closed in 1933, several attempts were made to reopen it in new locations, but all were very short-lived. As an organization, however, the Dil Pickle Club endured till 1943, when it formally disbanded. Its last president was Charley Wendorf. ¶ **Arthur Morrow Lewis** was one of the Socialist Party's most prolific and popular lecturers and pamphleteers in Debsian days. His *Evolution: Social and Organic* and *Vital Problems in Social Evolution* were published by the Charles H. Kerr Company in the 1910s and are still in print today.

ENDSVILLE
A Guided Tour of North Clark Street

LAST NIGHT TOM GANNON was talking about 'way back when Clark Street was one of the upper-class thoroughfares in Chicago. He wants to get it back to that. On the other hand, Gerry Gilbert wants to make his coffeehouse, The Red and The Black, the lowest-class Beatnik joint in town. It occurred to me that back in the Thirties I used to bring people slumming on Clark Street. What about all of us getting together and bringing them back to slumming here again?

To this end I hereby offer some material on Clark Street as the most fabulous street in Chicago. Let's take a little tour.

First we cross the bridge of the river that runs backward. Beyond that is the municipal building. Along with the courts, building departments, fire department and other offices is the traffic division of the police department. For a while the Chicago Avenue police precinct was lodged there.

Among these cops is one old-timer who was a habitué of the old Dil Pickle Club. Al Bibbe says he doesn't like being a cop. That's why he takes time off in disgust every once in a while to work on a material wagon for Consumers' Company. Whether he likes it or not, the kids learning the cop business think he's quite the old man when it comes to playing cops and robbers.

A couple of years ago he stopped a couple of thieves. They winged him in his gun arm. He reached in his left-hand pocket and came up with his little gun. The robbers are doing time now, and Al is still piling drunks in the paddy wagon. He says, if you need a cop, just stick your head out the door and holler. Clark Street is the best patrolled street in town.

Almost next door is the Thompson Building. It is now a monument to the vicissitudes of a bad labor policy. At one time Thompson's had thirty-three mammoth restaurants in Chicago, and God knows how many in other places. There used to be five on North Clark Street alone. It finally got so it took an act of God to get a cup of coffee from one of the country duchesses behind the counter. The one in the Thompson Building is the only one left on Clark.

The next spot of interest is historic. The Old Revere House was at one time the Algonquin of Chicago. All of the big-time actors of the 1890s lived there. I understand "After the Ball" was written there. It does not rate now as even a third-rate whorehouse.

Years back the Hobo College was at 437 North Clark. When we were thrown out of there, we'd go across the street to the Penny Cafeteria. The Hobo College is gone but the Cafeteria is still there.

A minor point of interest is the present site of the College of Complexes at 515 North Clark. It was chased there by avaricious landlords who wanted a little blood with their rent.

Kitty-corner from the College on Clark and Grand is a strip-joint where they don't take off their clothes anymore. A few doors north is Marco's, a new pizza parlor which supplies food and coffee to strippers up and down the avenue who can't live on pop and booze. The food is probably the best on the street.

Across from Marco's is The Red and The Black, the scummiest espresso house this side of Greenwich Village, run by a character name of G. Gilbert. Real Beatniks congregate here— the ones who wear real dirty beards and read real filthy verse.

In the next block is the Encore Theatre, which does only musicals. It is located on the historic site of the old French Casino. A. J. Liebling in his book *Second City* devoted more space to this joint than anything else. Rightly or wrongly, he seemed to feel that it typified Chicago.

On the next corner is the Liberty Inn. I was in the clink with its owner, Johnnie McGovern, some thirty years ago. It was a famous speakeasy then, but just another honkytonk now.

Across from it is the famous Ireland's Restaurant. Seafood is their specialty. Confidentially, you can get a better salmon steak at Rickett's on Clark and Oak for half the price. I haven't had anything decent to eat at Ireland's in twenty-five years. Yet they have been doing a land-office business since Chicago World's Fair Number One.

The most fabulous joint in all of Chicago comes next. About fifteen years ago a lady from New York had four hours to spend in Chicago between trains, so all I had time to do was show her our marvelous lakefront and Skid Road. This was eleven o'clock of a Sunday morning. At the Shamrock, the drunks from the night before were still at it. The lady leaned her back against the bar, shook her head and said, "I never saw anything like it." She is probably still talking about it back in New York.

Another time I took a couple of ladies slumming there, a drunk from two tables away joined us. After he told us about his numerous decorations in the war I informed him I was a pacifist. For this he was going to lick me. Naturally, being a pacifist, I tried to pacify him. The more pacific I got the more military he got. Finally I spotted the bouncer—a woman.

She says to him, "Go over there and sit down, you!"

"But this guy is unpatriotic."

"Go over there and sit down, I said."

He went over and sat down. I says, "Thanks, Lill." She stood five-foot-ten and was built like a Mack truck.

Frank O'Donnell, a bootlegger, started the Shamrock in 1934. I remember when it was a great big empty barn. If it doesn't net forty thousand a year now I'll sell you the College of Complexes for forty-nine cents.

O'Donnell also owns the Shanty across the street, and several others, I am told—all on Clark Street. One time I took a neighbor lady to the Shanty. A guy wanted to buy her a drink. Another one took a swing at him for being so bold. She just smiled sweetly while these two oafs were swinging at each other across our table. Her old man was a Golden Gloves champ.

There's an empty lot used for parking by the Cosmopolitan Bank. On that site used to stand the old Turner Hall. Old Man Appel owned it. He was the father of a movie star, whose name, I think, was Lila Lee. This was a famous hall. Gene Debs, John Peter Altgeld, Clarence Darrow and many other orators have graced its speaker's platform. The Dil Pickle Club was named for the free lunch in the Turner bar.

Two of the famous enterprises there were the Radical Bookshop and its in-house theater group, the Studio Players. A former preacher by the name of Udell ran the Radical Bookshop. He had a blind wife and two daughters, Phyllis and Geraldine. I think they started the Players after he died. Some very fine plays were put on there, with Phyllis Udell directing. Later they sold the bookshop to Bill Targ for ten cents a book. There were a number of rare first editions among them. Bill is now editor-in-chief for Putnam's, the world's largest book-publishing house.

A block and a half farther north is Bughouse Square. Its official name is Washington Square. There is a plaque stating that this square was donated to the city with the provision that a picket fence be maintained around it. Try and find the fence! Bughouse Square was for years the center of free speech in Chicago, and dozens of the greatest orators of all time have graced its soapboxes. Probably the greatest of them was John Loughman. A better speaker I have never heard anywhere. He'd make most of today's politicians seem like corny hams. Dave Tullman was another great soapboxer. Later he got deported to England. And there was one-armed Charlie Wendorf, who in later years spoke several times at the College of Complexes.

A few of the Bughouse Square old-timers are still alive. Bertie Weber, who had more brains than any of them, lives at Twin Lakes, Wisconsin. Jack Ryan runs a fix-it shop on Clark Street, near the College of Complexes. Jimmie Daniels is a corporation lawyer.

There is some talent left. The best of them are Bill Smith and John Carrol. Maybe I'm just getting old but I don't think either one of them could hold a candle to the old-timers. Maybe it's just that they have nothing to talk about. Besides, Bughouse Square is dead. Nobody wants to listen.

Further up on Clark Street, near Schiller, was once the home of the Temple of Wisdom. Of course it became known as the Pimple of Wisdom. I was in one of the first plays of my life there. As usual, the scenery fell down. Now they have the Second City Players at the end of Wells Street, where it meets Clark—one of the finest groups of players ever assembled in America.

Clark Street characters:

Mary Frances Riley has been playing the guitar and singing on Clark for twenty-five years. She is the author of two famous ballads: "Don't Clark Street Me" (sometimes called "Clark Street Blues") and "New Fool in Town"—both about Clark Street. She is now in her seventies, but she can still be heard

belting them out at the College on Fridays and Saturdays.
Give a listen to the immortal

Don't Clark Street Me
by Mary Frances Riley

Just because I came from Clark Street
Don't think you're too good for me.
Honey, I remember when
You were eatin' now and then.
Now don't try to Clark Street me.

When you turn away your head,
You make me wish that I were dead.
I can't forget the days that used to be.
When Kelly threw you in the jail,
Who's the gal that went your bail?
Now stop trying to Clark Street me.

Just because I came from Clark Street,
Don't think you're too good for me.
I'll admit your clothes are fine,
But they used to look like mine,
Now stop trying to Clark Street me.

Now you live on Lake Shore Drive,
You forget that I'm alive, but
I could spill the beans about your history.
And don't forget there was a time
When you bargained for a dime,
Don't try to Clark Street me.

And then there's Tom Gannon, who got the Whitman
Award for poetry once. He thinks us Beatnik poets stink. Ray
Olson makes his living as a commercial artist, but he does some
of the finest portraits in Chicago. Barre Heim, from Belgrade,
has played concert piano around the world. Joffre Stewart
claims to have been arrested more times than anybody in
Chicago. He is America's most persistent anarchist and pacifist.
He sports a beard and currently is anti-candidate for Vice-President of the United States on the Beatnik ticket. Bill Smith, who
has a flowing beard, is the Beatnik Party's Presidential anti-can-

102

didate. He claims to be the greatest authority on philosophy in the U.S. One character calls Smith a "philosopher by collection," on account of that is the way he used to make his living in Bughouse Square. He now runs a bookshop in the College of Complexes.

Janie Lewis writes plays and poetry. Gifford Heiser writes, paints, does Rorschachs, and drinks wine. Virgine Yount writes verse and leads the Poetry Nights at the College.

All of the above characters and more can be found almost any night at the College of Complexes, 515 North Clark—the most fabulous street in Chicago, or maybe in the world.

Abbot Joseph Liebling (1904–1963) is best known for his scathing criticism of the U.S. press (*The Wayward Press*, 1947, and *The Press*, 1964), and for his inspired chronicles of boxing (*The Sweet Science*, 1956). *Chicago: The Second City* was published by Knopf in 1952. ¶ Like most radical hoboes, **John Loughman** (died 1946) was—at least for a time—a member of the IWW; he played an important role in the Butte General Strike of 1919. For more about him see the texts by Farrell and Rexroth listed in the Bibliography. ¶ **North Side Turner Hall** was a regular meeting place for anarchist and socialist groups in the 1880s—Haymarket martyr August Spies spoke there often. During the 1910s and '20s a storefront in the building housed the **Radical Bookshop**, a popular IWW hangout frequented by Big Bill Haywood, Charles H. Kerr, Jim Larkin, Vincent St John and Ralph Chaplin (who also enjoyed playing chess in the Hall upstairs). Other frequent Bookshop visitors included Lucy Parsons, Emma Goldman, Vachel Lindsay, Carl Sandburg, Mary E. Marcy, Ben Hecht, Max Bodenheim, Kenneth Rexroth, Eunice Tietjens and Edna Kenton. Chicago's principal—perhaps only—outlet for the avant-garde poetry of France, Germany and the USSR in those years, the Radical Bookshop also had its own "little theater," the **Studio Players**, which survived the Bookshop's closing in 1929. A building rich in labor and radical history, North Side Turner Hall was demolished in the 1950s. ¶ **Udell**, a former Unitarian minister, and his wife Lillian (who wrote for the *International Socialist Review*), started the Radical Bookshop in 1914, with a large selection of books on consignment provided by the Charles H. Kerr Company. The Udells' daughters, Phyllis and Geraldine, helped run the shop and were also active in the Studio Players. Geraldine was a close friend of Harriet Monroe's, and served as business manager of *Poetry* magazine for twenty-five years. ¶ A well known Chicago bookseller for many years, **William Targ** (b. 1907) later moved to New York and became a major figure in the publishing world. In his autobiography, *Indecent Pleasures* (see Bibliography), he notes that his North Clark Street bookshop in the 1930s was frequented by "Bughouse speakers" and Wobblies. ¶ Many old-timers today recall one-armed **Charles Wendorf** as one of Bughouse Square's all-time greatest speakers. For more about him, see Keith Wheeler's article, listed in the Bibliography.

LET'S SAVE BUGHOUSE SQUARE!

Editor's Note: Chicago's Washington Square dates back to 1842, when land-developer Erasmus Bushnell donated a cow-pasture to the city, with the provision that it be maintained as a park. By the 1880s, German anarchists and socialists were using it for outdoor lectures and public meetings. By the 1910s it was, with the South Side Bug Club in Washington Park, the city's principal open-air free-speech forum, a status it maintained till the early 1960s.

HERE IS A WHOLE BLOCK of grass in the heart of the city of Chicago. But evidently grass is so common in these parts that the City Fathers regard it with contempt.

Did you know that the square in New York that bears the same official title is the object of a major political hassle there? One of the biggest wheels in the state of New York, Carmine DeSapio, is in danger of losing his own ward on account of Greenwich Village's Washington Square.

Did you know that there are no squirrels in New York's Washington Square? And no soap-boxers? New York's Washington Square has no great tradition of free speech associated with it. And did you know you can't even sit on the grass there? There ain't enough of it to go around.

But they've got committees, newspapers, Ma Roosevelt, Grandpa Moses and a lot of other celebrities fighting pro and con whether to allow traffic to go through Washington Square. They're not fighting about whether they'll let you sit on the grass, or whether they'll maintain washrooms. They're fighting just to save a bit of grass that you can't even sit on.

The other day I tried sitting on the grass in Chicago's Bughouse Square (Washington Square), but the stench drove me out. I've enjoyed sitting in that Square for over thirty years. I practically raised a kid on its grass. How many generations of squirrels I've fed there I can't count. But I guess I'm effete—I just can't stand the smell of stale urine.

Some fifteen years ago Chicago's City Fathers decided that it was too expensive to keep a policewoman there during the day, or even a washroom attendant during the night. So the washrooms are locked up, permanently. The Bughouse Square bums have to go to a saloon or use the walls of the washrooms for a urinal. Most of these bums are old geezers like me, on pensions. They lack the wherewithal to buy a glass of beer, and hardhearted beer-hustlers don't like non-paying customers to use the facilities.

New York's Washington Square has chess-tables for the oldsters. In Chicago's Bughouse Square, cops run the old guys in if they catch them playing cards on the benches. In the old days, Bughouse Square was full of women and children, but not now.

I remember on Sunday afternoons when the country-store Solons used to gather around the Bughouse Square fountain to discuss the events of the nation and the world. Most of them were slobs like me, but some great ones came down to talk with us lowly ones at times. Gene Debs, Clarence Darrow, John P. Altgeld are names the world will long remember. All three of them were habitués of Bughouse Square in their day. I wonder if they could stand the place now.

John Loughman was the world's greatest soapboxer. The only peer he ever acknowledged among public speakers was Darrow, whom he considered to be one of the three greatest speakers of all time. Jimmy Daniels is now a corporation lawyer. Will Wines is now big time in the Attorney General's office. Charlie Liebman controls over five million bucks' worth of real estate, besides his other holdings. Rube Menchen is another wheel as a real estate shark. James T. Farrell is now publishing his thirty-sixth novel. I could go on and on about the guys who got their start on Bughouse Square. But none of them are going to like my mentioning their connection with it now—because it stinks.

How about all of us getting with it? Let's start a committee to SAVE OUR BUGHOUSE SQUARE!

Editor's postscript: *The Janitor followed up the foregoing quasi-manifesto with letters to many old Bughouse Square "regulars" as well as to numerous public officials, including Mayor Richard J. Daley. The campaign, alas, proved unavailing. Far from improving the celebrated free-speech center, the Chicago Park District actually removed the washrooms and the benches, and let the place deteriorate still further.*

PROLEGOMENA TO THE
COMPLEX HISTORY
OF THE COLLEGE OF COMPLEXES

PEOPLE ARE ALWAYS ASKING how I got into such a business as a pseudo-intellectual bistro. It's like this. In 1945, I went to New York to sell my first novel. While there I got a job on the New Lots elevated structure, which is in the wilds of Brooklyn. One day when I wasn't doing anything else but painting the steel structure the boss went a block away and pulled on the cable I was standing on till it broke.

So I wound up in the hospital with a cracked heel, cracked pelvis, damaged ankle, and a broken back. For that the insurance company was ordered by the New York State Workmen's Compensation Board to pay me twenty bucks a week for the rest of my life. On account of they didn't think I was going to die very fast they figured this might run up into a chunk of money, so they offered to settle the case for six thousand bananas.

But the New York Compensation Board will not let slaves make settlements for lump sums unless they are convinced such slaves aren't going to try to drink up all the booze in the nearest saloon. As a consequence, the Illinois Rehabilitation Service was ordered to investigate me and my drinking habits. For some reason they concluded I could handle my money well enough to spread it around several bars at least.

My check from the insurance company was sent to the Illinois Rehab. I took some aptitude test to see if I had any competence to do anything other than push a paint-brush. Since I had flunked out of the eighth grade it was evident I didn't have brains enough to make a living at any truly intellectual pursuit. But since I always liked the taste of whiskey, and since I had graduated from Ozone University and was president emeritus of the old Hobo College, my aptitude score came out about ninety-eight percent for intellectual saloonkeeper.

Next I had to find a joint in which to install this neo-Dil-Pickle Club. Something happened to every one I picked out. There was a building down on Ontario Street I had my heart set on. Finally the agent told me the rehabilitator from the Illinois Rehabilitation Service was sabotaging me. The real-estate shark told me the owner of the building didn't want any broken-down housepainter trying to run a business in his building. There was no place else he could have found out about me except from the rehabilitator.

It has always been said of me that I am a very patient man. I will wait five minutes for anybody—that is, if they are flying in from Europe and can prove they had a rough crossing. But this was too much. Here was this government official sitting on my moolah and I couldn't do anything about it. Or at least, that's what he thought.

Sitting myself down to my little typewriter, I got busy. Starting with the governor I wrote to everybody I could think of who has any clout in the state of Illinois. In a few weeks the Illinois Rehab Service was getting letters asking, "What about this?"

What could the guy say? He said I was nuts. They even got me down to their headquarters where three of them gave me the third degree to prove it. For some reason or other their head-shrinker decided I wasn't nuts enough to be put away. So I wrote back to all these people I'd written to and said, "So they say I'm nuts. What's that got to do with my money?"

Finally, after waiting only six years, I got the check and bought a joint at 1651 North Wells Street. On January 6, 1951, the College of Complexes, Chicago's most distinguished institution of higher learning, opened its doors to eager throngs of students in search of intellectual and other stimulation.

Right away I was investigated by four sets of cops. The captain sent for me. He had my program for the week, it said the College of Complexes was the place where the literati lingered. He wanted to know what the "literati" was. I told him Men of Letters. He wanted to know if Yellow Kid Weil was a Man of Letters. I said the Kid had written a book, which ought to make him a Man of Letters, whatever else he might be. This cop also wanted to know if I was a Man of Letters. I told him I had written three books which, however, no one has yet published. Then he reached on a shelf in back of him and hauled down a dictionary. *That* scared me. It was the first time I ever saw a cop who knew what a dictionary was for.

Next I had cops from the precinct, other cops from the license bureau, and still other cops from downtown. Eventually

I was to find out I had cops from the Red Squad. They wanted to know just what, exactly, I was in business for. Even as stupid as I was, I finally figured it out: They suspected I was a front for the Communist Party. (The McCarthy Red Scare was on in full force.)

During my first three months I went in the hole fifty bucks a week. Came spring and I went to work pushing a paintbrush in Riverview Park, where I had worked many springs before. I did not make any money at the College for three years. For two years I worked to support the bartenders. One of them had his wife deliver her baby in a private room (all of mine were born in wards). I was out working eight hours a day while this was going on. My health gave out and I had to quit. I was taking in eight hundred dollars a week and losing money.

I tried to sell. A lot of people would have bought it if I had agreed to run it for them. But if I was going to have all the grief I sure wasn't going to let someone else make all the money. I guess nobody would buy it because they didn't think they could make anything out of it.

During that time the College of Complexes ran Pogo for President. We had our own campaign song, held rallies at the College, and generally made a lot of noise making fun of the powers that be.

We also had such renowned politicians and statesmen as Francis Sedgwick-Jell, Sidney Yates, Leon Despres, Archibald Carey and Douglas Anderson. Mr Jell was a very charming Chicago vice-consul for 'Er Majesty's government. Sid Yates was U.S. Congressman from the ninth district. Leon Despres was then a labor lawyer and a big shot in the Civil Liberties Union. Then as now Douglas Anderson was Illinois representative of Senator Paul Douglas. Archibald Carey came to tell us about what happened when he was U.S. delegate to the United Nations. Judges Jacob Braude and George Quilici also spoke at the College.

All debates, speakers, entertainment and other College activities were announced well in advance in our monthly four-page publication, *The Curriculum*, subtitled "The Official Neurosis of the College of Complexes."

Among the eminent professors who addressed our classes, I remember Bess Sondel, Paul Schilpp, Herbert Blumer, and W.

Willard Wirtz. They were all speakers at the forum during my first two years in business. They may be names you never heard but in their own fields they are tops. The first three are Ph.D.'s. Sondel has ten books to her credit and is one of the country's most renowned consultants on communications. Schilpp, who talked on pacifism, has published eight books, and besides that he is a preacher, psychologist, and philosopher. Herb Blumer was All-American twice, professor of sociology in several universities, editor of the leading sociology magazine, and chairman of the Institute of Social Science. The last-named fellow, Wirtz, has something to do with the working class now—an underpaid job as Secretary of Labor in Washington, D.C.

That first couple of years we didn't have many writers at the College. Novelist Jack Conroy, one of my best friends for many years, loaned me his mailing list of three hundred names and M.C.'d our first meeting. He had won a Guggenheim Fellowship years before. Conroy returned to the College many times over the years; one of his talks was titled, "Do the Angry Young Men and the Beat Generation Speak for All of Us?" Poet Ken Nordine, well-known on radio and TV was another frequent reader at our mighty citadel of learning. Herb Bailey was writing only medical articles then. He was yet to make Krebiozen, the so-called cancer cure, one of the most controversial subjects in America.

And then there was Nelson Algren. After many years I have finally figured out what was wrong with him: He was scared to death of people. We threw a bash for him once at the College that lasted from two in the afternoon till midnight. The day before he called up saying he couldn't be there because he had to go to Toronto. I told him, "In that case we won't have the party." He said he'd come.

In the meantime I had adapted one of his stories for the stage. It was called "A Bottle of Milk for Mother," from *The Neon Wilderness*—Chicago in the raw as only Algren can paint it. It was well-rehearsed and a big hit. The whole Chicago writing community turned out for the party. Algren left after an hour.

Jack Conroy said to me, "I'd like to blast that guy. Imagine running out on us." I said, "I'll blast him," and I did, too, in an open letter published in the July 1956 issue of *The Curriculum*.

One alleged writer seemed to impress a lot of people around and about. His name was Max Bodenheim. Everywhere he went he was drinking up everybody's liquor. Figuring I had more of the stuff on hand they tried to wish him off on me. Knowing this character of old, I said no. These people had to do something to get Max off their necks so they got the brilliant idea that I would throw a party for him. I still said no. Then they brought him over and decided to let him sell the idea himself.

"Max," I says, "I've known you for twenty-five years. You've put your feet under my table and your scummy lips around my bottle. You were the only person I knew when I hit Greenwich Village trying to get a novel published. You told me you 'didn't want to be bothered with the lower classes.' So now you can just walk back to New York."

Some weeks later a reporter called up from the Associated Press and said that somebody had stuck a shiv in Bodenheim. He wanted to know, what did I think of that? All I could reply was that I couldn't understand why someone hadn't done it twenty years ago.

Politically, and in every other way, the speakers at the College ran the gamut. Four aldermen, two judges, a congressman, twelve preachers, twenty university professors, a United Nations delegate, a candidate for Mayor, a couple dozen lawyers, the same number of authors, the world's fastest runner, a big-league pitcher, Wobblies, Democrats, Republicans, Commies, socialists, anarchists, Trotskyists, pacifists, atheists, Catholics, Protestants, Humanists, Rightists, Black Nationalists, integrationists, single-taxers, Zionists, hypnotists, poets, nudists, cops, ventriloquists and Beatniks by the dozen held forth there. As already intimated, some of our speakers were almost respectable.

Among the preachers we had in those years were William Baird, Paul Schilpp, Homer Jack, Edwin T. Buehrer and Archibald Carey. Homer is now the head of the Committee for a Sane Nuclear Policy, better known as SANE. E. T. Buehrer ministers at the Third Unitarian Church in Austin, which has always had forums of its own. Arch Carey was so much in demand in those days we never could get him to speak again, although he kept promising he would come when he got time.

Considering that he kept up a law practice and preached a sermon every Sunday it's not so surprising.

Other speakers who helped raise the educational level of greater Chicagoland at the College in those years include Burr McCloskey, Fred Thompson, Edward Marciniak, Joe Giganti and Virgil Vogel. Agitator, muckraker and a good friend, McCloskey has been a consistent supporter of the College all through the years. Thompson, another old friend, is the IWW's historian. Years ago he spent time in the clink out in California under the "Criminal Syndicalism" law; in other words, he is one of the hundreds of Wobblies who went to jail to get better conditions for workers all over the U.S. Marciniak was editor of *Work*, organ of the Catholic Labor Alliance. Giganti is a Marxian socialist who teaches economics at DePaul. Vogel is a socialist, too, but his special field is the history and culture of American Indians.

There's one guy who never spoke at the College, but I can't neglect him in this history. He came around and cased the joint before I had been in business three weeks, and dropped in occasionally thereafter. He was an agent for the Internal Revenue Service. His name was Swede Sullivan, and he told me that if I ran the joint like I was running it then I would not have to pay an entertainment tax. More about this later.

Around forty years ago when I first came to Chicago, "Yellow Kid" Weil was a name everyone knew. He was the world's greatest confidence man. He said so himself. It was said that he got his name because he liked to dress in yellow, but I never saw him in anything yellow in my life.

In his book the Kid says he never "took" an honest man or a friend. It may be true—in his book. I don't know. I don't know if the Kid would recognize an honest man if he saw one, but I do know he hasn't any friends. And I also know that his brother sold his entire household for some money he borrowed and didn't pay back.

Anyway, the Kid had a little racket he worked on every forum in Chicago where he spoke. This is the way he did it to me: He was a well-advertised speaker, the house was full, but Yellow Kid didn't show up till a half-hour past curtain time. Then he came up with some story about having to go to a hospital or something and that he had to have so much money or he couldn't talk. Some way or other he always knew almost to a dime what you were going to make off the crowd, and he took it all.

At that time I had another fellow getting my speakers. I told him to offer the Kid a flat tenspot for an appearance after he had run this gimmick on us once. But I'm afraid my program chairman was no match for the Kid. It wound up costing me fifty dollars.

From then on I contacted the Kid myself. I told him flatly that the stipend was ten dollars, that he was the only one I ever paid, and that there was no use trying to con me. The Kid looked up at me with his innocent brown eyes from his full five feet and said plaintively, "Why Slim, you know I wouldn't con you. I'm your friend."

After that the Kid made several appearances without any trouble. Then a third party came on the scene. My publicity man decided he would have the Kid hold a press conference. Reporters, photographers, and even a television camera arrived at the College. After two hours it was obvious that the Kid wasn't going to show up. Knowing his passion for promptness unless he was setting up a mark, I figured he must be in jail or a hospital. Four hours later he's down at the television station getting himself taped. He has some story of course, but I didn't listen to it. I know it's a con.

That night he was supposed to talk at the College and he showed late. But that time I had a substitute. All my boys were telling me in the middle of the lecture that the Kid was outside in the bar. I told them to leave him out there. After sending several envoys the Kid finally deigned to come in and ask me if I wanted him to talk. Since the substitute speaker had finished, I told him to go ahead if he wanted to and he did.

After an hour he came around and asked if I wanted to see him. I asked him what would I want to see him about? "That ten," he replies. "What ten?" "That ten you always give me for speaking." "I didn't promise you any ten tonight." "But you always give it to me." "Not when you run a con on me."

He was a master con-man all right. Whether he was the greatest or not, I don't know. But he had a whole hassle of the boys and girls worried about what he was going to do to me. Some were afraid that he was going to sue me if I didn't give him that ten. Next day the public relations man called up. He was worried, too.

I asked, what could the guy do? "Why," says the p.r. guy, "he might really sue you." "Man, what a publicity man you are," I answered. "If you can't get that on the front page, I'll fire you. Ought to make headlines on a slow day. 'Yellow Kid Swindled by College of Complexes.' Can you beat that for a story?"

Of course he had to admit it was a story that would be worth a lot more money than the Kid could recover in any suit. And of course he couldn't be induced to sue me under any circumstances. Later, when I told another con-man how I'd conned Yellow Kid Weil, he laughed so hard he almost fell off the bar stool.

Like all educational institutions the College of Complexes had blackboards. In fact the first thing we did was paint all the walls black and leave out lots of chalk, making the whole room a blackboard. Naturally this gave everybody an impulse to write. I was determined to perpetuate mankind's greatest achievement: the penning of doggerel on the walls. I put up the first signs myself, simply to encourage art. One read, "It's against the law to sell booze to drunks, minors, spendthrifts, lunatics and all distracted people. Let's see you prove you ain't." And on the ceiling I wrote, in letters two feet high, "No television, no jukebox, no 26 game—just beer, booze, and bull-oney." If I ever get back in business I'm going to put it back there (but this time I'll change the 26 game to hi-fi).

None of the things I put up were particularly clever. I'm not a clever person. What I did put up came from the heart. Like the one that got the most attention: "One more genius and I'll cut my goddamned throat." That place was full of geniuses. Or so they told me, one after another, every day.

Putting a few gags around was just to stimulate the thinkers in the house. You know, like "I can do better than *that*." And they did. Some of the things these geniuses put on the wall have gone around the world. People could make a living copying the stuff from the walls of the College and selling them for greeting cards. "Work is the curse of the drinking class" is said by some to have originated with Oscar Wilde. But we don't even know the name of the genius who put up "Learn to complain without suffering."

Here are a few quotations that endured throughout all the years I ran the joint.

Against stupidity the very gods themselves contend in vain.—Friedrich Schiller

My candle burns at both ends. / It will not last the night. / But ah my foes, and oh my friends, / It gives a lovely light.—Edna St. Vincent Millay

The moon's gone dim, / The sun's turned black. / I loved him / And he didn't love back.—Dorothy Parker

I don't care if your name is Napoleon, get your hands out of my blouse.—Zsa Zsa Gabor

In addition to lectures, discussions, and humorous sayings on the walls, the College had lots of great entertainment. The College Players put on plays by Shakespeare, Chekhov, Ibsen, Tennessee Williams, Jack Gelber and many others. They even produced one of *my* plays. All the actors said it stunk. But everybody laughed!

Music was another regular feature. Big Bill Broonzy, now a legend, used to sing at the College on Wednesday nights. Several times a month we had folk songs, jazz concerts, jam sessions. Ella Jenkins sang and played for us many times. Bob Gibson and Studs Terkel dropped in now and then. There was a story in one of the papers recently stating that Bob played his banjo in the place for a couple of bucks a night, but it isn't so. Like all the other folk singers, he did it for kicks. He could pack a house even then.

Let's put in a plug here for one of the greatest entertainers the midwest has ever produced. It says in *Who's Who* that Studs Terkel is a radio commentator, producer, actor, playwright, lawyer and author, and has won many awards for narrating here and abroad. He's also one of the sweetest guys I've ever known.

One of the greatest personages that ever came through our

doors was Mary Frances Riley. She was what is known as a *busker*. The word comes from *buskin* which the dictionary says is a half-boot that actors wore. In the old days when actors were out of work they'd do an act on the street and pass the hat. Mary had been doing this for years on Clark Street. She mentioned to me once that she almost got caught in a raid on an opium den in Frisco in 1917. She had gone into this place, played her guitar and sang, but before she could take up a collection she had to crawl through an alley window to get away from the cops. She hadn't known it was a hop joint.

And so it was that Mary Riley wandered into the College of Complexes one night during the first six months we were in business. To the great benefit of several generations of students, she stayed on as one of our regular faculty. She kept the joint jumping for four hours every Friday and Saturday night. She never received any pay except what she collected in the hat. This procedure obviated the necessity of collecting an entertainment tax for the government. Or so we were repeatedly assured by Swede Sullivan of the I.R.S. Nine years later Mary was still coming to the College on weekends. So were other buskers dropping in off the street.

Clark Street Mary, as she was known, used to sing the old college songs for the kids—and practically any other song anyone had ever heard. Many people told me she couldn't really sing. That was because she sang the songs in such a way that anybody could sing along with her. There was no use arguing with these people. As a matter of fact once a year we would put Mary Riley on the official program to sing a few arias from operas. Her voice in those days was mellow and powerful.

Mary was also quite a poet. She would read her poems at our poetry sessions which we had whenever I felt rich enough to afford one. Two of her many poems she had set to music. They were called "Don't Clark Street Me" and "New Fool in Town." These songs were so popular that she sang them at least twice every evening by popular demand.

By the way, this was well before Mitch Miller and the "sing-along." Red Quinlan, who recently quit as boss of WBKB television, was thinking seriously of putting the College of Complexes on the air, and one of the things he insisted on was that Mary Riley be the star. We auditioned the show. The station sent over an artist to sketch the joint, so they could reproduce it in the studio. We were scheduled to take over a spot one night a week. But Quinlan evidently was having the same trouble with the home office then as now. The network president bought a million dollars worth of old movies and made him put them on the air instead. There wasn't time left for our live show.

Even so, someone from the College was on TV almost every week. In fact, some producers of shows called us up when they wanted to fill in a spot in a hurry. They knew we always had interesting people around.

At times my critics and well-wishers thought they had to caution me about how to stay out of trouble. One way was to be careful who I had speaking in the joint. But I have always had the conviction that anyone running a free-speech emporium couldn't deny the platform to anyone with something valid to say. Consequently, when I scheduled the Communist Party candidates, the prophets of doom predicted dire consequences. I think there were more cops there that night than there were customers. Everybody was there except the Gestapo. The Communists, Claude Lightfoot and others, told how they were followed night and day. Round-the-clock surveillance by two FBI agents. They were harassed on their jobs and off. Even their kids were followed to school and back.

As everybody knows, the format at the College of Complexes was for an expert to give a speech of the evening. After that the floor was thrown open to questions and discussion.

That night, when the time came for me to give my spiel, I figured I might as well get killed for a lion as a lamb. "This joint is dedicated to Free Speech," I said. "We are in the business of dispensing free speech to anybody who wants to listen to us." I told how I had been fed Karl Marx with my first spoonful of oatmeal, and how my father had been a socialist and a radical all his life. I had belonged to the Industrial Workers of the World, or Wobblies, which was the most radical labor organization the United States has ever known. It's true that I never bought the Communist movement, but I was and still am a Marxist by definition.

I went on to postulate that this was basically a fascist country, and that one of these days the government of the United States would close up the College of Complexes and put me in a concentration camp. "The concentration camps will be full of Free Speech, and that's where we'll likely end up. But until that day we'll continue to have free speech in the College of Complexes."

To emphasize my contention that the U.S. was already basically fascist I pointed to the chairman of the meeting. It was his boast that he had been thrown out of the United States Army during World War II because he said we were fighting the wrong people (at that time Russia was our noble ally, if you remember). Yet no FBI men were following *him* around. Nobody was trying *him* for sedition. Nobody was harassing *him* so he couldn't make a living.

After the meeting, the boss of Chicago's Red Squad came up to me and said, "Slim, we'll never bother you from now on."

I have no doubt that I have been under surveillance many times since. But for nine years there were no cops or FBI men in evidence at the College.

Another little program we had, which I was warned about, didn't turn out so well. At that time Bob Merriam was raising hell in the City Council about Chicago's corrupt police force. So I got Charles Liebman to give a talk on "Chicago's Criminal Cops." Charlie was an old friend from Dil Pickle days. He had also been one of the officers and builders of the Chicago Civil Liberties Union. Having been raised in a slum neighborhood he was, and still is, rather rabid about cops.

That was in March of '54. Next year, when the College moved to 862 North State Street, the police department refused to transfer our license on one pretext and another. After two months of runaround I applied for a hearing before the Chicago Liquor Commission. One of the exhibits was our *Curriculum* listing Charlie's speech on the program.

Around forty people showed up to be character witnesses for us. One of the best was Will Leonard of the *Chicago Tribune*. When my lawyer asked him if he'd ever seen any minors in the place Leonard answered, "Yes, my two girls, eight and ten. I took them in there to show them the place. Why doesn't the police department go close up some of the rotten clipjoints in this town? I'm the nightclub editor and I know what is going on."

One of the indictments was that we had "pornography" and "sex lectures." Thinking to ameliorate this charge my lawyer asked me if these sex lectures weren't kind of watered-down anyway. What could I do with a house full of reporters? I answered, "Not if I can help it."

At one point in the trial the prosecutor stated that "A tavern is not the place to have discussions." I pointed out that Julius Caesar and Marcus Tullius Cicero met in a tavern to decide the fate of the world.

After about a month the Liquor Commission ruled in our favor. But it still didn't get me my license. Some way or other I couldn't get it off the police commissioner's desk. I was told later he had a suspicion that I was anti-Catholic and he was just giving me a bad time. If I'd known that, I would have had some of the Catholic friends and speakers of the College talk to him. Some influential people did contact the Mayor and at last the license was granted.

Incidentally, I was interviewed by a police captain in the Commissioner's office. Can't remember his name. Anyway, he pulled out a stack of correspondence two inches thick devoted to the case. People had been writing about it to the Mayor and the Commissioner. Probably no one stuck his neck out further for us than Herb Lyon of the *Tribune*'s "Tower Ticker."

This is as good a place as any to tell about some of our Collegiate institutions. One of them was the "Met and Married Club." It listed all the people who met in the College of Complexes and got hitched. One of the girls married my accountant. Her daughter married one of the bartenders. And they are all living happily ever after (I hope).

We finally had to give it up. The "Met and Married Club" ran out of space on the wall. What started this, I seem to remember, was the "Available List." This was on the wall like an application for employment: name, age, sex, height, weight, marital status, occupation, and financial rating. One young lady wrote "flat busted" in all brackets. A male listed his occupation as "stud." He got four phone calls the next day.

Outside, on the College's front door, was a painted sign that read: "Through these portals pass the most odious offal in the world: Our customers." When the Syndicate bought the property we occupied on State Street, they sent an emissary around to ask us to remove it. They thought it was in bad taste. So did we—but the sign stayed.

It wasn't more than three weeks after we moved to State Street that a hoodlum came in. He rasped, "What ya t'ink yer doin'? You t'ink ya can move into a neighborhood and not see anybody? Around here ya got to cut somebody in."

I replied that I was running a legitimate business; why should I "see somebody." He answered, "Who ya t'ink yer kiddin'? Looka dat joint across da street. Da cops closed it. Look at dat one up da street. Closed."

"What's that got to do with me?" I ventured.

"Hey, don't get smart wid me. If you wanna stay in business you better see my boss."

This was too much. I lost my temper. I said, "Okay fellow, I don't know who sent you and I don't care. Very likely you can move in here and take over. I don't have any clout and I haven't any muscle. So take it over. I know you won't last here a month. And I'm not going to run it for you. I'm going back to housepainting."

Without another word he left. In about a half-hour he came back and said his boss said it was all right. I could run the place. Big deal. Before the day was out his boss came around and very nicely told me he wouldn't bother me. Nor did anybody else while I was in that neighborhood.

However, a number of salesmen came around and mentioned they were bosom pals of the right guy in the neighborhood, adding that it would be real smart of me to buy from them. Since I was satisfied with most of my purveyors I didn't do business with any of them, except one. That was a linen supply, and they proved to be unsatisfactory. I tried to get somebody else to take the account but nobody wanted it. I was told that everybody was afraid to take it. After some time the supplier I had had on Wells Street came around to see what was the matter. I told him he hadn't shown up so I gave it to the man nearest. He took the account back and everybody was happy.

Recently I looked up one of my favorite customers of the old days on Wells Street. He says, "You remember that debate Phil Myers had with Tom Gannon on whether man would ever colonize Mars? You remember how I got up and blasted them? One of them was a housepainter and the other was a clerk in the customs house. What did *they* know about it? As an engineer I was in a position to know that man wouldn't even get to the moon in two generations. I sure made those fellows look pretty silly."

I said, "Yeah, I remember."

"I sure am smart," he laughed. "Last week I sold some equipment to land on the moon."

When you're writing a diatribe like this from memory one is apt to forget his old friends and the people he owes the most to. One of these I barely mentioned. That is Alderman Leon Despres. He and Charlie Liebman were on the old Snivel Liberties Committee board with me, back in the Forties. How many favors I owe either of them I couldn't even begin to count.

I used to kid Leon about his comic-book campaign before he became Alderman. Personally I don't care a hoot whether my kids read them or not: clean ones, dirty ones, or even educational ones. So when he would come around to the College and speak once a year, he got his revenge by telling the assembled multitude what a clown I was. Maybe I should have disputed it but I couldn't think of any good arguments against him. But let me say for the record: Leon Despres is one of the finest men this city has ever produced. There is nobody in the City Council or anywhere else as dedicated as he is to the welfare of the people of Chicago. More than that, he is a fine lawyer, a humorist, and like most good politicians, a first-rate ham. He was also one of the best friends the College ever had. Any time we needed a helping hand he was right there. I remember climbing in his twelfth-story window once, in the Temple Building. It was like old home week. He put his arm around the dirty painter and said to my partner, "Take care of this guy. Don't let anything happen to him. He's valuable."

Now I ought to tell you about the people I can remember who would *not* talk at the College of Complexes.

Harold Urey kept promising me for two years he'd come over. Several times he apologized for not setting a date. Finally he asked if he couldn't beg off. After all, Nobel winners are pretty much in demand. Characters such as Ed Ryerson, William Caples and Laird Bell politely refused. I guess they were afraid of being found dead in the joint. Or maybe somebody might think they were Communists. The same must have been true of a number of top labor leaders. The only one who came at all, from the upper echelons, was Pat Greathouse. Another exception was my old friend Sid Lens—a labor leader and a good one. He's also the author of a number of very fine books. Once a year he would always find time to give us a talk. Sid contributes to a number of think magazines and is an authority on Latin America.

Dr Andrew Ivy was scheduled to speak once, but found out that we dispensed booze. He was afraid he'd have to drop his membership in the anti-saloon league. His mentor, Anton J. Carlson, would have been glad to come, but his doctor forbade it. For years Douglas Anderson tried to get Paul Douglas over to the place but senators seem to be almost as busy as aldermen. Alva Tompkins would have liked to come but Olivet Church, of which he is pastor, is evidently too close. Then there was a guy who used to write copy for the City News Bureau, who seemed to think he was an authority on prostitution and such things in Chicago. He wouldn't come to the College either. Name of Kogan.

But that's all right. I never held it against anybody who didn't want to blat in my bistro. Some of them think it's a childish pastime. And who am I to argue with them? Tastes differ. Personally, I think *baseball* is dizzy.

But what *does* gripe me are people who give me the runaround. One of these was Joe Lohman. This was before he got to be Cook County Sheriff. He was just a prof at the University of Chicago back then. As if I was an old buddy of his he'd say, "Slim, I just can't make it this week. You know how busy I am." This went on and on. Finally even I caught on that he had no intention of ever coming around.

When I first started the College on Wells Street, there was an outfit getting in the news quite a lot for some reason or other. They called themselves the North Central Association of Secondary Schools and Colleges. I knew then that the only thing the College of Complexes lacked was accreditation. So I wrote these people. It was a nice note, of course.

After a couple of months I wrote them again. This second letter wasn't quite so nice. I gently reminded them that I had written them a letter and the dirty stinkers hadn't given me the courtesy of a reply. This time they sent about four yards of forms for me to fill out in quintuplet. Not only that, they made a lot of other fabulous stipulations.

Well, this provoked me. I kind of opened up on them and told them what I thought. Anybody who would expect the president emeritus of the Hobo College to read those forms— let alone fill them out—was a dirty this and that.

After still more correspondence they agreed to present me with a certificate if I would give them the platform for an evening. Naturally our forum was open to everybody. These two young fellows went to a lot of trouble working out a show for the night. The material was extraordinary, and because they were educators it probably wasn't too hammily presented. But at the end of their program they presented the College with the certificate. We had it framed and kept it for years. (Alas, somebody later stole it.)

The handsome certificate proclaimed to the world that the College of Complexes was a "fully discredited institution whose academic standards are far below normal." So all was forgiven. I hope those boys are doing well.

And how, you ask, did this historic document get stolen? Well, eventually the point was reached where it became fashionable to steal something from the College of Complexes. Only once in the early history of the College do I recall anyone asking for souvenirs. On that occasion I dug up a College pennant, my business card, and the College diploma. I have since heard that our pennant is flying in bars as far away as Johannesburg and Singapore. My business card makes people take a second look, and the College diploma says, "This creature by name _____ has completed all of the proscribed courses and copiously qualifies as a prodigious underachiever."

Once a year we had Commencement exercises. This was when our speakers commenced to live. At the College, we didn't graduate students, we graduated the teachers. Everybody who graced our platform during the year got a diploma conferring the degree, Bachelor of Complexes, Maximum Cum Laudanum. One year Judge Braude couldn't make it so we awarded him one *in absinthia*. Incidentally, that's his joke, not mine. But the most important part of the whole affair was the Bacchuslaureate Address. Now *that* was a work of genius—I know, because I always delivered it myself.

Now is the time to say something about the people who really made the College of Complexes what it was in those early years. Great names come and go. But what keeps a pseudo-intellectual bistro alive is the pseudo-intellectuals—the ones who are there every day, or at least every weekend. Various segments of the population like baseball, bowling, dancing, music, fishing and fighting; some of them even like children. This is all right. But people who like to kick ideas around are called kooks, or Beatniks, or something equally derogatory.

Probably the College of Complexes owes more to Tom Coffey and Tom Gannon than any other two people. I personally know they have been punching the bag in intellectual bistros for the last thirty years. Many a time when I needed a speaker in a pinch one or the other saved the day. Tom Coffey has shared my addiction to verse since the 1930s. (He could bring down the house reciting *The Raven*.) Before the Depression, he was a painting contractor. But when tenants couldn't pay, why should landlords decorate? So Tom painted with workingclass slobs like me. People we worked for often asked, "Isn't he colored?" "I don't know," I replied, "I never asked him."

George Reynolds, who got thrown out of the army for saying we were fighting the wrong people, now owns and operates a twenty-four-flat building in Vancouver, B.C. Jack Lanagan is a poor man's folk singer at Aspen, Colorado, at last report. Don Walker had to quit fooling around and stay home with his three kids. Phil Myers is a big shot in the customs service but he comes around once a year looking for some of the old gang.

Jo Fowler who debated Guy Bush on "Will Sex Ever Displace Night Baseball?" is raising monsters at Crystal Lake. Her ex-husband, Garvis Fowler, became a schoolteacher at forty. He was the College chairman for several years. Mike Elliot, Dean Natkin and Ben Jones used to win a lot of the College Quiz Programs. Ben is the head of the Cleveland office for Continental Casualty. Dean is protecting the taxpayers' money working for Cook County Welfare, and I can't find Elliot. Pat Scully, who directed several College plays, is cooking hamburgers for Moody's Pub.

Some of these folks stayed on for years while others drifted off to other things as newcomers drifted in. The later history of the College, however—including two of its all-time biggest newsmakers: the saga of Miss Beatnik of '59 (Gnomi Gross) and the 1960 Beatnik Party anti-election campaign (with College habitués Bill Smith and Joffre Stewart running as anti-candidates for anti-President and anti-Vice-President)—will have to be told another time. It's time now to wrap this thing up.

In June of 1957 we opened a branch of the College of Complexes at 139 West 10th Street, Greenwich Village, in New York City. (James T. Farrell was one of our speakers there.) Early in 1959 we bought another place at 638 Broadway in San Francisco's North Beach. After leaving a ten-thousand-dollar deposit there for six months we had to give it up because we could not get a satisfactory lease. (Frisco real-estate agents and landlords were hostile to anyone with Beatnik sympathies.)

I say *we* in these cases because my manager in the Chicago College was putting a good share of her earnings into the Colleges. Like me she was a hillbilly; her education was two-and-a-half years shorter than mine. After I tried out a half-dozen geniuses for manager in Chicago she took it over and made us some money. If you came to the College in those years you knew Margaret. Her last name was Lachnovich.

When the Syndicate bought the property on State Street they tripled our rent. Several people told me to go back to Old Town, where the College had started. But I was too smart for that. We'd come from there because everybody had to make an expedition to get there. Instead, we went and bought a building over at 515 North Clark Street. Margaret put her earnings into it and some besides. That was in January, 1960.

My reasoning was that I had started the College in two very bad locations. Within a couple of years bookstores and art galleries began to move in alongside of us. Shortly the whole neighborhood was booming. This was because we spent four thousand a year on promotion. This time, I figured, we would reap the benefit of our own building instead of having a landlord raise our rent for increasing the value of his property. But we live and learn.

Then a guy from the Internal Revenue Service came around. He said we owed entertainment taxes for the last nine years.

In March of 1961 the Internal Revenue Service sold the New York College of Complexes for three-hundred and sixty dollars.

In May of 1961 we closed the Clark Street operation. People did not want to come to that badly rundown street. In five years I'm confident I could have built up the business and cleaned up the area. But the IRS would have taken everything I made as fast as I made it so it would have been a losing battle.

As of January 1st, 1963, the Internal Revenue Service said I owed them one hundred and one thousand, seven hundred and twenty-eight dollars, and one cent.

And so I went back to my trade as housepainter. No more steel. Passed my sixtieth birthday last November. Ain't the man I used to be. That slugging with a roller for eight hours a day gets me down. Besides, I can't keep up with the young stuff.

Got a couple of offers to start the College at a salary and commission. Well, we'll try it again.

It isn't all fun, but anything beats working for a living.

One of America's most readable proletarian writers, Missourian **Jack Conroy** (1899–1990) is best remembered for his 1933 novel, *The Disinherited*. He coedited the *Rebel Poet* in the 1920s, the *Anvil* (1933–35) and in Chicago, with Nelson Algren, the *New Anvil* (1939–40), which published early work by Margaret Walker. Though he lived most of his life in his hometown of Moberly, Missouri, he remained in Chicago for twenty years. IWW-oriented in his youth, he was briefly a member of the Communist Party, but returned to his original Wobbly outlook in later years, and was an enthusiastic supporter of the revival of the Charles H. Kerr Company. Douglas Wixson's excellent biography (see Bibliography) unfortunately neglects Conroy's association with the College and his long friendship with Slim Brundage and Fred Thompson. ¶ Born in Akron, Ohio, **Burr McCloskey** was for many years a militant rank-and-file organizer in the rubberworkers', steelworkers', and mineworkers' unions, and has remained a strong voice for a truly radical labor movement. The Lynds' *Rank and File* (see Bibliography) devotes a chapter to this phase of his activity. McCloskey is also a poet, essayist, short-story writer and novelist; his *He Will Stay Till You Come: The Rise and Fall of Skinny Walker* (1978), is a vivid fictional portrayal of the emergence of industrial unionism in the 1930s and '40s. A powerful and popular speaker, he has addressed the College at least once a year since it first opened its doors in 1951. He lives near Chicago. ¶ IWW organizer, editor and historian, Canadian-born **Fred Thompson** (1900–1987) is best known for his book, *The IWW: Its First Fifty Years* (1955; revised and expanded, 1976), but he also wrote scores of important articles on IWW and labor history, as well as much of the union's best promotional literature. His posthumously published autobiography, *Fellow Worker*, compiled by Dave Roediger (see Bibliography), is one of the finest Wobbly memoirs. The principal reorganizer of the Charles H. Kerr Company in 1971, Thompson served on its Board of Directors from that year on, and as its president in 1986–87. ¶ Born of Sicilian-Jewish parents in Chicago Heights, **Joseph S. Giganti** (1904–1986) was an early member of the Communist Party, active primarily in its Italian-language branch, and in labor defense (as Chicago director of Sacco-Vanzetti defense). In 1928 he was expelled as a "Trotskyite," much to his amazement, for he in fact supported William Z. Foster's faction and had given little thought to the Stalin/Trotsky dispute. Eventually he did join the Trotskyists' Communist League of America, and was briefly active in the Revolutionary Workers' League. An independent socialist in later years, he served as president of the Charles H. Kerr Company from 1973 to 1986. ¶ Lifelong socialist **Virgil J. Vogel** (1918–1994) was one of the first members of the Congress of Racial Equality (CORE), and took part in its first Chicago restaurant sit-in in 1943. After receiving his Ph.D in History at the University of Chicago, he specialized in Native American studies. Among his many noted works in that field is the classic *American Indian Medicine* (University of Oklahoma Press, 1990). With Fred Thompson, Burt Rosen and Irving Abrams, Vogel helped reorganize the Charles H. Kerr Company in 1971, and served as its president from 1971 to 1973.

One of several versions of the College diploma

126

A JANITOR'S GUIDE
TO THE COLLEGE OF COMPLEXES

THIS SPIEL IS ABOUT the internationally infamous Beatnik bistro and educational institution known as the College of Complexes, alias "The Playground for People Who Think." It opened up in 1951 and it's still going strong nine years later. The author happens to be the owner of the joint, as well as the janitor.

People are always asking, "Where did you get the idea?" And I answer, the College of Complexes ain't nothing new. They had tea-rooms with discussions in them in Chicago around the turn of the century. In my time I can remember the Temple of Wisdom, the Gold Coast House of Correction, the Lower Depths, the Intellectual Inferno, the Seven Arts, and there were others I can't recall offhand. Most of them were just discussion clubs. But the Dil Pickle Club had plays and dancing besides the lectures. All the College of Complexes is, when you get right down to it, is the Dil Pickle with a bar added onto it.

And where did the name College of Complexes come from?

That goes back to Martha Biegler, a great old woman who ran a rooming-house to end all rooming-houses at 337 West Chicago Avenue. When you got thrown off of every decent newspaper in the United States, when you couldn't climb a six-foot ladder to paint a ceiling any more, you got a job washing dishes and moved in with Martha Biegler. Sometimes you paid rent and sometimes you didn't. A broken-down reporter by the name of Red Terry dubbed her place the House of Complexes. I just borrowed the name.

Before you even set foot in the College you will notice some brilliantly colored paper signs on the windows: "Fallout Cocktail—Prevents having mutants for heirs." "Castro Cocktail—Will grow hair on your chin." Then there's the sign on the door: "Through this portal passes the most odious offal on this orb: Our customers."

Inside, over the bar, chances are there's a god-awful art exhibit. Across from it in black light are the accumulated gags of nine years of scribbling. (Anyone can have chalk to write on the blackboards that infest the place.) Some of these are classics such as, "It is better to remain silent and be thought a fool than to speak and remove all doubt," by Abe Lincoln. And some, like "Work is the curse of the drinking class," attributed to Oscar Wilde, have gone around the country since appearing on our walls. As far as we know, the following are original. Some Beatnik or other just writes them and forgets them.

Flunk out now. Avoid the rush.

Chicago has the best politicians money can buy.

I don't care whose last supper it is—no I.D., no wine.

If you must matriculate on the floor, go next door.

World War III: where all men will be cremated equal.

We hate everybody regardless of race, creed, color, or sex.

Are you working on the solution, or just part of the problem?

Aside from the gags on the walls the rest of the room looks a lot like any other bar. Of course there will be the usual habitués. Some of them have beards. Some are professors or social workers or employees of the State's Attorney's office. While I am writing this, bearded Beatnik Bill Smith is talking to a psychology professor from Indiana U. and a statistician from Continental Casualty. They are kicking the gong around on why the American theater stinks.

Now you pass through a double swinging door. There is a lecture going on. If you don't keep your big flabby mouth shut, you'll get thrown out on your ear. That's what we have two rooms for: one for jokers like you who want to blabber to your date, and the other for people who want to listen to an expert on some question so they can show him the error of his ways later on.

Next month at the College we will dedicate Monday night as Radical Night. All of the little radical outfits you have never heard of, like the Socialist Labor Party, Anarchists, Trotskyists, Wobblies and others will be here. The Communist Party refused to attend. Maybe there's too much heat on them. Or maybe this joint is on their shit-list.

Tuesday nights we are supposed to have the Mighty Brundage Players doing Blackouts and Improvisations. Since this is another one of Bill Smith's brainstorms and Bill is a Beatnik, it is likely nothing will come of it, unless somebody like yours truly makes it happen.

Wednesday night is Beatnik Night all through next month. Bill Smith, the Lordnik of Beatnikism, will not only challenge the bourgeoisie, the mossbacks, pseudo-liberals, pseudo-intellectuals and pseudo-pseudos to debate at two paces, but will also give you a rundown on why the Beats reject this and that. This and that consists of such things as Religion, Science, Art, Show Business, Newspapers, Sex, Family and you and me. In case you don't know it, that's what makes Beatniks—they reject everything.

Poetry Night is every Thursday. Old poets and new. For years we have been trying to promote poetry. Although not much happened, somehow it cost a lot of moolah. But now the Beats have made poetry popular. Maybe young Beatnik Kent Foreman is reciting his "Chicago." Maybe an old beat-up housepainter called Tom Coffey is reciting Poe's "Raven." Could be someone else is reciting something done in Greenwich Village by a Beat named Dan Propper, the "Fable of the Final Hour." Could be yours truly is only shooting Dan McGrew or cremating Sam McGee. Listen and join in.

Friday night is the big intellectual night. You might find a delegate to the United Nations, a physician, a congressman, an economist, a preacher, a famous athlete, an advocate of birth-control, the secretary of the Juvenile Protective Association, an Anarchist, a librarian, or just an alderman or candidate for mayor of Chicago. Whoever it is, the speaker is guaranteed to be an authority on the subject.

Speakers are given up to one hour to unload the wisdom they have prepared. After that, the audience has a half-hour to throw questions at them. Meetings start at nine p.m. Usually the speaker of the evening takes between a half and three quarters of an hour. When the question period is over the audience shows the poor expert how wrong he is. Politicians, do-gooders, physicians, atomic scientists, lawyers, philosophers, all get their come-uppance at the hands of the characters in the audience who know everything. The speakers ain't got a chance. Even so, some of them have been coming back every year for nine years.

Whatever the lecture is on Friday night you will learn something. Very likely you will also be entertained by the wags who get their kicks out of giving the experts the business. If you were lucky enough to hear Judge George L. Quilici read Ferlinghetti's Beatnik poetry you would have been enthralled. Nobody does a better job of reading in the United States—and we have had some professional readers here from stage, screen, and radio.

Next week Jim Kelly is going to tell you about "The Mafia's $600,000,000 Tab You're Picking Up." (Look back and count those zeroes again; that's what the Mafia picks up in Chicago alone.) And the following week George Watson, Dean of Students at Roosevelt University, is going to explain "Why There Are No Revolutionists on Today's Campuses."

Saturday nights at the College are for the lighter element— people who want something frothy that ain't going to make them do too much thinking: a Quiz Program, for example. Everybody in the house gets a couple of tickets. Some character reads quiz questions out of a Quiz Book. Then another dirty character, like maybe me, goes around and points at you. When he does this, you are supposed to answer the question the geek asks you out of the book. If you can't answer, I go on to the next joker, and keep on till somebody answers it. You lose a ticket every time you can't answer a question. Finally, when there are only four tickets left, a panel is made of the survivors and everybody gets their revenge. The presumption is that if you get on the panel you know everything. And to prove it you get a College of Complexes pennant with Quiz Winner stamped on it, thereby demonstrating for all posterity that you've got brains, on account of the only way you can get one of these pennants is to win it (although we do have plain old College of Complexes pennants for sale). Anyway, if you are smart enough to answer more questions from the audience than any of the other three, you also get a free bottle of scotch (bar scotch, of course—the other is too expensive).

If you'll look up the word "symposium" you'll find that it means "drinking and discussing." It goes back to Socrates. We don't encourage too much drinking while a meeting is in progress. In fact we don't encourage too much drinking at any time. You can't in an operation of this kind. If I had to put up with a lot of sloppy drunks like my neighbors do, I'd go back to housepainting.

Of course we sometimes have trouble with somebody who already had too much when they came in. As far as that goes, we have trouble with some of them when they're cold sober. First I explain to them that the speaker of the evening has done a lot of work on a serious lecture and serious people want to listen to him. I also explain that if they're civilized they can tell him where he's wrong if they want to wait till he gets through.

That usually works. If it doesn't, I just tell them to keep their big mouths shut. If that doesn't help, I ask them if they're going to be slobs all their life. And after that there's only one thing to do: call a cop. I was open two months when I had to throw the first guy out. Never even knocked his glasses off. (I was bouncer at the Dil Pickle in the old days.) Anyway, in about an hour I had four sets of coppers around. This character had all of his friends call up the station. He was supposed to have been hospitalized, blood all over the place, and all that. The cops said I was supposed to call them when there was any trouble—it's on my liquor license. Besides, I ain't so young any more.

Other activities on Saturday nights are demonstrations of hypnotism, talks on Nudism, "How to Make Out on a First Date," or "How the Law Affects Sex," by a divorce lawyer. Sometimes on Sunday nights there is a jazz combo.

Last but not least is our concert pianist. He plays Bach, Beethoven and Brahms in between, after, and before everything. His name is Barre Heim. He has played the classics in most of the capitals of the world on concert tours. By the time this is published he may have taken off for greener pastures. You can't keep a genius in a Beatnik operation like ours for long, so we expect to lose him any time. As of now he has taken a vow of poverty, grown a beard, and plays what he likes for the assembled multitude. This guy could make fifteen grand a year on the tenderloin but he'd rather play for nix for the Beats. They give him food for his soul instead of dough that he just has to buy drinks with anyway. The only way he can play for the squares, says he, is to stay drunk. But please do not buy drinks for this character! When he gets two drinks in him he's so far out we have to send up a ladder after him.

This is the Playground for People Who Think, the only intellectual nightclub in America. There are lots of other joints that cater to baseball fans, racecourse fans, stage fans, fight fans and everything else. Why shouldn't there be one place in the good old U.S.A. where people who have a thought north of their navel once in a while can get together and talk?

Minors are admitted if accompanied by their grandchildren.

As Brundage indicates, Chicago in the 1920s/30s had many other forums besides those he mentions here and elsewhere in this book. Sophie Fagin, in her thesis on the subject (see Bibliography), describes over sixty forums that were active in January 1937, and her list is far from complete. Especially well-attended were the forums, usually held weekly, at settlement houses and social service centers such as Hull-House, Northwestern, and the Abraham Lincoln Center. Most radical organizations, including the IWW, the Universal Negro Improvement Association (followers of Marcus Garvey), the anarchist Free Society Group, the Socialist Labor Party, the Communist League of America, the Irish nationalist Connolly Club and the Proletarian Party, held regular forums, often attracting audiences numbering in the hundreds. Many local colleges, and a few churches, also had forums. Ethnic groups—Italians, Poles, Germans, Swedes, Yiddish-speaking Jews, and others—often had forums in their own languages. In warm weather, moreover, there were several open-air free-speech forums besides the celebrated Bughouse Square and Bug Club—one near Navy Pier, for example, and others at various times on West Madison Street and on Roosevelt Road.

An invitation to the College

HAIL AND FAREWELL
TO ALL YOU SQUARES!

Editor's note: The first part of this text is an example of how the Janitor welcomed people to the College and introduced the evening's featured speakers. The second part records his concluding remarks following the general discussion.

GOOD EVENING, all you squares out there. You are now making the scene with the cats at the College of Complexes, also known as The Playground for People Who Think, or the Beatnik Bistro. The College, a unique tavern club, has been described by Alderman Leon Despres as "the last real open forum remaining in Chicago."

Tonight, three of the College's Beatniks are going to "sound the cat." The cat in this instance is Professor Lawrence LeFave of the University of Indiana. After he blasts on the subject, "Are Beatniks Just Clowns, or Thorns in the Status Quo?" the three Beats are going to try to put him down. These hipsters are: our bearded pianist, Barre Heim, the best-traveled Beatnik in Chicago; Julie Workman, freelance writer and Beat waitress; and Slim Brundage, janitor.

The College of Complexes is a gathering place for a wide variety of way-out characters, some of whom practically live here. Hipsters, artists, Beatniks, writers, judges, aldermen, college students and Bughouse Square refugees tune in here for yak-yak and a glass of beer. Politics, poetry, sex, the price of marijuana, current events or what-have-you—any and all subjects get a good kicking around at the College every night.

The College of Complexes operates in the tradition of the soapbox, the cracker barrel, the corner saloon, the opium den and the Bug Club in Washington Park. The nightly programs are interlaced with lectures, hip and square, as well as skits, book reviews, community singing, hypnotists, quizzes and other light entertainment, all aimed at demonstrating what is going on in this swinging world.

Besides its varied programs, the College is noted for the humorous and thought-provoking sayings that are chalked on its walls. So if you're so square you'd rather look than listen, glim the walls for their wit.

For a copy of the complete monthly program of the College of Complexes, write to our box number.

And now for our program. We turn the microphone over to Prof. Lawrence LaFave of Indiana University.

You ready, dad?

* * *

The program you have just heard is true. The names and opinions of the characters—and they *are* characters—have not been changed to protect anybody. They *never* are changed at the College of Complexes. The discussions, programs, quizzes, debates—everything at the College of Complexes is real, bona fide, unfixed. No sham, no shame, no fake.

Everyone is invited to come to the College of Complexes to listen, to participate, to lead a discussion on any and all subjects. Everyone has the opportunity to speak his piece at this famous tavern club, one of the most stimulating and entertaining places in the Midwest.

Every Friday and Saturday night there are discussions on current topics, after which "Clark Street" Mary Riley leads the community singing.

Tuesday night is Radical night.

Wednesday night is Beatnik night.

Thursday night is Poetry night.

Barre Heim, concert pianist, plays the classics every night.

Also visit our current art exhibit—oils, pastels and miniature sculptures by Ray Olson.

A visit to the College of Complexes is a unique and varied experience. You will always come back for more.

Eat, drink and be stimulated—at the College of Complexes!

'College' Man Enters Race

Beatnik Candidate Runs For President of U. S.

Pittsburgh *Courier*, Chicago Edition, March 5, 1960

II.
RAVINGS

THE JANITOR
OF THE
COLLEGE OF COMPLEXES
CHALLENGES
THE
MILITARY-INDUSTRIAL
COMPLEX

THE

Curriculum

Meetings start 9:00 p.m.

OFFICIAL NEUROSIS OF THE COLLEGE OF COMPLEXES
Slim Brundage, Janitor
Minors admitted if accompanied by their Grandchildren

515 N. Clark St., Chicago | Month of March, 1960

Thurs 3rd - "DOES BEATNIKISM HAVE A PHILOSOPHY?" Bill Smith, Pied Piper of the Beatniks, will delve into the eight areas of this question.

Fri. 4th - "THE CHICAGO POLICE DEPARTMENT AND ITS TERRIBLE RECORD OF CIVIL LIBERTY VIOLATIONS." Donald P. Moore, member of the Board of Directors of the American Civil Liberties Union and author of "Secret Detention By The Chicago Police," will explore the relationship between the record of the police in civil liberties and the corruption in the Department.

Sat. 5th - "YOU, TOO, CAN BE REINCARNATED!" Addison Brown, who is experienced in the field of reincarnation, will inform you about living life over and over.

Thurs. 10th - "ARE BEATNIKS IMMORAL?" YES! says Slim Brundage, straitlaced guardian of North Clark Street; NO! says Wild Bill Smith, honest bookseller.

Fri. 11 - "DO EUROPEANS HAVE A HEALTHIER ATTITUDE TOWARD SEX THAN AMERICANS?"—Alba Ryan, who has certainly been around, will give us her viewpoint on this thorny question.

Sat. 12th - "THE PSYCHOLOGY OF SEX."—This is the talk given by John Carroll that has played to S R O crowds throughout the country (no kidding). Well acclaimed. Come early for seats.

Thurs. 17th - "BEATNIKS, ANARCHY, AND ST. PATRICK" will be given a goingover as Bill Smith continues the Thursday Nite Beatnik sessions.

Fri. 18th - "DID THE U.S. LOSE WORLD WAR II?" YES says Burr Mc-Closkey; NO! says George Leighton, as both tangle in the debate on issues which everyone has been devouring since V J Day.

Sat. 19th - W. C. FIELDS AND CHARLIE CHAPLIN. Ed Hoff, president of the Roosevelt University Film Society, will present three Fields classics and one Chaplin. The Fields movies are "The Fatal Glass Of Beer," "The Pharmacist," and "The Barber Shop." The Chaplin entry is "1 A.M.," the only movie he made in which he is the only actor.

Thurs. 24th - "ARE BEATNIKS OPERATING IN THE PAST TENSE?" YES says John Carroll, always thinking of the future. NO says Bill Smith, always searching for a present.

Fri. 25th - "WILL THE U. S. HAVE SECOND-RATERS IN THE NEXT OLYMPICS?" Jesse Owens, immortal Olympics track star, will give us a preview of what we may expect at the forthcoming international competition.

RADICALS

TWENTY-FIVE YEARS AGO in the Dil Pickle Club, we'd kick the gong around on this and that. We'd wear out one subject after another. Then about two years later some wise guy would publish the cogent and startling thoughts which he just discovered and we'd forgotten about.

So I prognosticate that in a year or two some brain will discover that "all radicals ain't dead yet."

Just as a gag, I'm always saying I'm the only real radical around this joint. The reason is that I got Karl Marx with my first spoonful of oatmeal. I just missed getting myself fourteen years in stir by being in the Wobbly hall in Centralia, Washington, in 1919.

My old man campaigned with Gene Debs for social security, child labor laws, eight hours for women, old-age assistance, unemployment insurance, public ownership of utilities and women's suffrage. If the good people of that day didn't openly hate him they thought he was a dreamer. But he and a million other dreamers wrote the Socialist Party platform of 1912. Out of twenty-three planks in that platform, eighteen have become the law of our land.

Now, the good middle-class kids who inhabit the College of Complexes can laugh at songs we sang, like "The White Slave," "We Have Fed You All for a Thousand Years," and "Solidarity Forever." But who made the soft beds they lie in? Where would they be today without the damned radicals like my old man?

So what has become of all the radicals? What happened to the forty open forums Chicago used to boast? Why are there no more than three open-air forums in the whole of America? Have all the frontiers been won? Are people no longer interested in making this a better world?

John Alexander, a sociologist who attends the College, suggested that the radicals were operating in a different era. Sure. Most everything that was radical in my youth is accepted now. The types who took to the soapbox were the ones who battled on the economic front. But the radical is still with us. He is still going to jail for what he believes. But he ain't where he belongs. That's why we think he's dead.

Webster says a radical is "One who advocates radical and sweeping changes, with the least delay." My own definition is, "One whose avocation is the building of a better world."

The Curriculum, July 1956

DIL-PICKLE CLUB

**Thru Hole in Wall at 858 N.State St.
Down Tooker Alley to the Green Lite
Over the Orange Door.**

Sunday, November 10th

at 8:30 P. M.

*42nd Anniversary of the hanging of
the Chicago Anarchists*

Memorial
Meeting

SPEAKERS:

Lucy Parsons
Hypolyte Havel
Nina Spies
George Schilling
John Loughman
Dr. Ben L. Reitman, Chairman

The Haymarket Riot May 1st, 1886 and aftermath was one of the most important events in the history of the American Labor and Radical movement. It was the beacon to the shorter workday. ■

"Prof." Jack Dunham of whom it 's said "He's 90 per cent brains" and Dr. B. Dasannacharya M. A., Madras; Ph. D. Munich; F. Inst. P. London will alternate in a series of lectures Wednesday evenings.

Plays and Dancing Friday and Saturdays

A Dil Pickle Club announcement printed on
Jack Jones's Dil Pickle Press (1929)

LITTLE DREAMERS

EVERYTHING WE SEE was at one time a small dream in someone's head. Daedalus dreamed of wings to fly the sea. Our brothers dream of a little flight to the moon. Kufu's dream was a mammoth pyramid and Frank Lloyd Wright's is a mile-high building. Our fathers dreamed of an eight-hour day and we are hollering for six. My mother dreamed of a world without the burden of children and my daughter will fight like hell to have some. Jesus dreamed of freedom for the subject peoples, and Gandhi's Satyagraha is making that dream come true.

Everybody has dreams. Your value as a human can be determined by the worth of your dreams. A Babbitt of North Avenue once said to me, "What does this guy J. Robert Oppenheimer know about living? He never made more than eight grand a year in his life." Just like the Berkshire hawg who raises his snout from the trough to grunt, "What does the honeybee know about good swill?" Poor indeed is the man whose dream is no more than the getting of geldt.

But may I implore you to make your dreams come true. For dreams without achievement are as empty as the Babbitt's dreams are crass. Dr Oppenheimer is a scientist whose dreams are the achievements this world will use whether he makes ten cents a year or not. And even if he ends his life in a concentration camp he will always have the satisfaction of knowing he made at least *some* of his dreams come true.

But let's leave the dreamers of the big dream and get around to the little dreamers like you and me. My people dreamed of a stump ranch at the other end of the Oregon Trail. Your father dreamed up some little gadget that would make this world a better place for you to live in. Your people and mine are not found in *Who's Who*. They only dreamed the little dreams.

But what would this country be without the little guys with the little dreams? Our frontier would be the Potomac instead of the Pacific. We'd still be looking into the south end of four- footed transportation when we moved north. There are some million patents in the patent office. Each of these little dreamers with his patent has contributed something to the sum total of the world's greatest civilization.

We build a monument to the Unknown Soldier and don't even know who invented the internal combustion engine. We give our biggest rewards to movie stars and executives of mammoth corporations. Yet, without the army of little dreamers who have made this grandiose civilization, these characters would have no one to entertain, or any corporation to exec.

from the booklet, *Ravings* (slightly abridged)

SCHIZO CERTIFICATE

To all ye who pass these portals and enter into the COLLEGE OF COMPLEXES know ye that we, The Right Honorable President and Dictator of all Schizos, ruler of all Paranoics, Maniacs, Neurotics, Manic Depressives and all other persons who have left the realm of sanity:

That we have by virtue of our exalted office entered this creature into the Loyal Disorder of Schizophreniacs, and she, he, or it, will show little or no sanity on pain of absolute expulsion and eternal abjuration.

Be it known to all and sundry in this College of Complexes that the undersigned_____ is a full fledged Schizo of passing Quality.

_____President

The official College Schizo Identification Card

EXCERPTS FROM THE BACCHUSLAUREATE ADDRESS TO THE COLLEGE OF COMPLEXES GRADUATING CLASS OF 1955

HERE ARE WE, living in a soft fat land where the wealth of the world is piled to the heavens. The richest of kings of antiquity lived like a mujik compared to the humblest of us now. Most of us have never been hungry, have never been cold. And just lately it has been decreed that such should not happen unto the least of us, from the cradle to the grave. So what happens? We develop ulcers.

Who are we? We are the darlings of the gods who revel in the wonders of a world we never made. "We have not toiled at the fishing when the sodden trammels freeze. Nor worked the war boats outward in the flush of the rock staked seas." What do *we* do? We get ulcers.

What are we? We are the creatures a hundred generations toiled and sweated and died for. We sit here tall and straight, well educated, and at our ease. We are the acme of things accomplished. We are the dreams come true. Our progenitors dreamed down slavery and they dreamed down kings. They toiled and fought and bore the oppressor's lash that some day their kind might come to this. What do *we* do with it? We get ulcers.

Where are we? This is the continent bordered by two oceans to which our fathers fled. They killed off the buffalo, the Indians, and everything else just to make a place for us to cultivate our ulcers in peace. Now that we have inherited everything they dreamed for us, we are not content. One of our leaders considered that the Rhine was our border and another the coast of Asia. That leaves a small segment of the world we do not claim as ours.

No large voice has been heard crying out against this policy of world conquest. If we cared, we would not now have soldiers in forty-nine countries throughout the world. Like imperial Rome we are extending the *pax Americana* throughout the world, whether the peoples like it or not. Is it any wonder we have ulcers?

When are we? We are at the apex of history. We have inherited all that a dynamic society could give us. If we are to believe Oswald Spengler, it is downhill from here. Another society will arise and displace us.

What are we going to do with our heritage? That is the problem that we must decide. You who are going forth from this room have that responsibility more than anyone. Not only are you the highest type of mentality this city affords, you are also the highest human. If you were not a person of courage you would not be here, because of society's criticism. If you were not a person of humor and intelligence you would not be here because of the hypercritical audience.

Even though we are a few voices crying in the wilderness it is, because of our heritage, our bounden duty to make that cry.

The Curriculum, April 1955

YOU'RE KIND OF CUTE . . . . AND
YOU LOOK LIKE YOU MIGHT BE INTELLIGENT TOO !
SO
MEET ME MON. ☐ TUES. ☐ WED. ☐ THUR. ☐
FRI. ☐ SAT. ☐ SUN. ☐
AT
COLLEGE OF COMPLEXES
862 N. State St., Chicago
"The Playground For People Who Think
Meetings start at 9 p.m.

An invitation to the College

FOURTH OF JULY SPEECH

ALTHOUGH SAM JOHNSON said patriotism was the last refuge of a scoundrel, Webster defines it as "devotion to the welfare of one's country."

The great minds who wrote the Declaration of Independence made a monstrous squawk about such things as patriotism, justice, consanguinity, equality, liberty, rectitude and some ephemeral thing called the pursuit of happiness.

Justice: Ben Franklin said, "We must all hang together or most assuredly we will all hang separately." The Tories of that day, who comprised half the population, considered these revolutionists as business buccaneers who would get their just deserts if they were ever tried in an English court.

Consanguinity: These patriots appealed to the people of England not to prosecute a war against them on the grounds of blood ties. That denotes a certain intolerance for those not belonging to their racial group.

Equality: The first thing stated in the Declaration is that all men are created equal. But were the Indians equal? Were the Negroes equal? Were even the women equal?

Liberty: With twenty-five percent of the population in slavery, how much liberty was there?

Pursuit of Happiness: These were the same jokers who pushed the indigenous natives out of their homeland to pursue their own happiness on foreign soil.

Will anybody contend that these characters weren't patriots? By either Webster or Johnson most of them could qualify. They were a hassle of snobs who thought no slob should vote unless he owned at least one mule. Franklin wanted to know, "When a man takes his mule to the voting polls, who will vote, the man or the mule?"

Patriotism, justice, equality, liberty, rectitude and even the pursuit of happiness are not enough. Today we live in the world of faster-than-sound transport. This is the world where four men can wreck a civilization ten thousand miles away. This is the world where patriotism (by either Webster or Johnson) is no longer a virtue. It's a vice we can no longer afford.

The revolutionist of today must inscribe on his banner not

the Liberty, Equality and Fraternity of that day, but the cry of Charity, Magnanimity, and Brotherhood of today.

What is needed now is not the old consanguine brotherhood of me to mine, but brotherhood, charity and magnanimity to the four-fifths of the world who are non-white. For our own survival we must forswear this over-devotion to "our own" country. How about a little charity for the three-fifths of the world who don't know where their day-after-tomorrow's breakfast is coming from?

The Curriculum, August 1956

Beatniks Hold Convention in Coffee Shop

Antipresidential Candidate Of Beat Party Selected

BEATS' DRAW UP PLATFORM: ABOLISH WORK

Pick Cool Beat In Hot Contest

Take Care, You Political Candidates, Beatniks Ready to Make Their 'Move'

Bill Smith Is Beat Party's 1960 Nominee

Way Out Beats Are Holding a Convention Too

Beatniks Run Bearded Man For President

July 1960 headlines from the Cairo *Citizen*, Mt Vernon *Register-News*, Woodstock *Sentinel*, Champaign-Urbana *News-Gazette*, Danville *Commercial News*, Rockford *Star*, Freeport *Journal-Standard*— all published in Illinois—and the Gary (Indiana) *Post-Tribune*.

PERSPECTIVE

THIS IS A DIATRIBE about perspective. When your dear old manic-depressive was a mere four feet high, the teacher told him the story of the peas in the pod. Since they were green and the house they lived in was green, the whole damned world had to be green.

"But nobody goes hungry these days," said the dogooder's wife. When I reminded her that three-fifths of the world's peoples don't know where tomorrow morning's breakfast is coming from, she replied, "I guess I meant the people here in the city." Just a little green pea whose world is the green opulent city she lives in. A college degree didn't help.

"Thou shalt not kill!" says Joe DiLeo delivering a book review that pleas for peace. Then he cries about careless hunters who kill each other. He doesn't squawk a word about killing poor defenseless deer that never did anybody any harm. Deer ain't green so they don't count.

"But God made deer for man to kill!" What is this colossal ego of man that lets him think some divine being made every living creature just for his sport?

"Good, kind, beautiful man?" Phooey! He robs the bee of its honey and the sheep of its coat. What he can't enslave he kills. As a final act of horror he nurtures "God's creatures" to maturity just to murder them for their skins. And not even to keep him warm. He murders these innocent critters just to decorate the back of Miss Googoo McGam.

"The most horrible thing in the world is the stockyards." Try to imagine yourself a helpless animal being hauled to the slaughter. But *you* don't do the killing. There is no blood on *your* hands. But you and I will have nice crisp bacon for breakfast. It's a beautiful green world as long as someone else does all the killing for us. "The wonder is that man can smile dreaming his ghostly ghastly dream," says Sir Richard Burton.

So why am I always hollering for a better world? Because I inherited a world where my ancestors killed off all my enemies. They even killed all the devil-gods my fathers prayed to. The only way I can pay for my inheritance is to try and leave a better world for those who come after me.

The Curriculum, January 1955

WHO BEAT THE BEATNIKS?

THE OTHER DAY out in Frisco, one of the upper classes wanted to know how I could stand Beatniks. I tried to explain to him that despite a rating with Dun and Bradstreet, I was an old beat-up Beatnik myself. "What you got against them?" I asked. "They don't like to work," says he. "Do *you* like to work?" says I. He didn't reply.

Everybody wants to know, "How come Beatniks?" And I'm the boy who ought to know. Most Beatniks come to bohemia and live for a spell and go back home to the fatted calf. I was born in it. I didn't run away from home. There wasn't no home to run away from.

In Frisco they have declared open season on us Beatniks. The tough punks from across the Bay want to work out their hostility on somebody easy, so they come to North Beach. "Dem intellectools just read books. Dey can't fight." So they beat up on the Beatniks, and the cops arrest the Beats for getting in the way of the punks.

It wasn't so different back in the old days around Chicago's Dil Pickle. The same punks were coming around to hammer up on us. Well, most of 'em went away sadder and wiser, on account of a lot of us came out of the radical movements. We were bricklayers, steamfitters, painters, piano movers, and gandy dancers, along with the kids from the suburbs.

But when I look at these kids today, they look the same to me. The same sloppy clothes. The same defiance of conventions. The same patter of art, dance, theater, and literature. We called ourselves bohemians and hobohemians. So do they, refusing to accept the term Beatnik. Being an old Wobbly, I doubt the courage of this attitude. In our day when they called us Wobblies, instead of crying "We ain't no such thing!" we proudly adopted the name as a token of defiance.

Call me radical, call me subversive, call me Wobbly, hobo or Beatnik—I'll answer and be proud of it. The day will come when we'll throw these names back in your teeth and make you eat them. And if this be treason, make the most of it.

But what made us come to this beat-up, back-alley warren of rooming houses? Why does your kid come to North Beach,

146

Greenwich Village, or the Near North Side? Maybe you gave him Brooks Brothers, Ivy League and a Cadillac. Why has he run away from all that money can buy him? Man, it frustrates the hell out of you. Why does your daughter run away to live in a five-dollar room? Why does she take the dough she slaves for to buy beer for some half-assed poet?

All I know is what the kids tell me. Janice is a poor babe whose old man ain't got but a million or three. She can keep busy drawing plans in the old man's office. She can play sailor girl at the yacht club with some local yokel. And she's way out there with status on account of her old man has more bananas than any other cockroach on the landscape. But who needs it?

Will Wines says, "Give a man food, clothing, shelter. Everything else is satisfaction." All the green stuff in the world ain't going to put Janice where she belongs. She's had it, man. Her beautiful, sterile home ain't no answer for hunger of heart and a place in the sun. So she sleeps on the floor in somebody else's pad. She tries to paint pictures. She gets odd jobs as a beer jockey or soup-slinger. Sometimes she skips dinner because the restaurateur wants moolah and she's fresh out. All she has to do is go home to the fatted calf. But what does she do? She marries a beat-up bar-beast with no talent at all.

Sammy's old man runs a store that nets twenty grand a year. They live in a sixty grand shack in one of Nelson Algren's suburbs, "where the sky is always smokeless, the churches are always tidy, homes are pictures out of Town and Country, and the people are stuffed with kapok. . . . The streets of the tenements seem to breathe more easily, as though closer to earth, than do these sinless avenues."

So Sammy comes to the College of Complexes and tries to eat off what he makes taking pictures. Expert photographers starve at it, but anything beats working in the old man's store. Besides that, he can take off his shoes in the College. And when he gets too frustrated he knocks his fist through the washroom wall. (Wait till I catch the son of a. . .)

But why? *Why?* Here you've been breaking your back all these years to get the kid the works. You want him to be somebody. Ain't that it? You poor slob, what have you given him? Status! That's what you have been fighting for all these years,

147

But the status you've given him is empty. What kind of status can he buy with a fancy address and a Rolls? All he can do is impress somebody. Who? The kids he grew up with? The poor slobs like you across the tracks? Who needs it? This may spell status to you but he ain't with it. Besides that, he's got a natural urge to rebel against parental authority. That's the way he's asserting his adulthood.

In Chicago's Beatnik area, there are other kinds of status. Not the kind you buy with outer accoutrements. But the solid kind that comes with accomplishment. Here he can talk, or paint, or write, or poetize. Maybe he's from nowhere on all of it. But it still gives him a status you never gave him.

A friend of mine is worried about his daughter. Will she wind up supporting some uncouth, unwashed bum down in the Village? Will she come back home? Well, that depends on how tolerable you make the home. Or whether they have a chance of making it here.

I was talking to another old beat-up Beatnik yesterday. Now he's a colonel. We compared notes. One of the old gang is the brains in an attorney-general's office. A couple are working on their third million. One is a world-famous novelist and one was a movie star. And a lot of them are in the booby hatch.

Your guess is as good as mine, Pop.

The Curriculum, July 1959

BEARDING THE LIONS

These Two Beats
The Men to Beat

Kennedy and Nixon may not realize it, but they will have the beatnik slate to contend with in November.

Bill Smith and Joffre Stewart—the beats' choices for President and Vice-President — have set up campaign headquarters in a saloon at 515 N. Clark.

"We're campaigning in the M⁻ ʼwⱼ ᵗ ʰ ₐₗₗᵤ̇ ᵢₜ' ᵗʰ ₛₒ̇·

became fashionable — were nominated last week by 135 delegates to the national convention of the Beatnik Consensus party, held in a Greenwich Village (New York) saʼⁿⁿᵖ

Chicago Daily News, July 27, 1960

YOUR LIVES ARE RIGGED

Editor's Note: *This "Raving" was provoked by the government's and newspaper editorial-writers' response to the news that major TV quiz shows had been rigged.*

THERE'S SOMETHING WRONG in America. There's something *wrong* in America! Or maybe it's just with me. I can't get through my thick head what all the hollering is about on the TV quiz shows.

Who got hurt? Did the sponsors who spent millions on the show lose anything? Did the contestants? Did you? What is the crime these producers are accused of? Rigging a show to make it more entertaining for *you*! What in hell did *you* lose? Your faith in human nature? I lost mine ages ago.

But one English major hollers that there should be a dividing line between fact and fiction, even if it is a TV show. Supposing somebody rigged up the newscasts, he says. Pretty soon we couldn't believe anything. My God, what does he want to do, put all the public relations men out of business?

Newscasts are rigged every day all over the country. Eighty-five percent of all the news in a paper is supplied by p.r. men. And their business is rigging the news the way they want you to swallow it. What do you think the College of Complexes hires one for?

Now don't get me wrong. We don't believe in rigging anything. At the College, our quizzes have never been rigged, and never will be as long as I have anything to do with them. And despite some fancy offers, nothing else has ever been rigged in the place.

But your *lives* are rigged. The *Readers' Digest* is fact, not fiction. Yet the International Ladies Garment Workers' Union paid some cluck three thousand bucks to place an article in it. Pure fact. Nothing but. I know one writer who makes his living writing "fact" articles for this type of mag.

He got twenty-five hundred from a manufacturer, plus what the magazine paid him, for a lot of "facts" about a product. It later turned out that the product was not only harmful, but outright dangerous. Was that information rigged or not?

Everybody in the world knows that our State Department is trying its best to foment a war in Laos so they can send our kids over there to kill Communists. Everybody knows it except you smart Americans. And the reason *you* don't know it is because the newscasts are rigged by the State Department. The War Department, the F.B.I. and the Atomic Energy Commission are rigging news-stories every day. They are for the express purpose of getting us into a war of total destruction. But what do you care? It doesn't interfere with your entertainment.

When I opened the New York branch of the College of Complexes, I was told I would have to "pay off." I didn't believe it. (You wanta buy a good saloon, cheap, in New York?)

Like Diogenes with his lantern, I went up and down New York streets looking for an honest man to stand up with me and fight that corruption. The lawyer for the Liquor Dealers Association says, "Mister, I wouldn't even let one of my members stand with you." These are the freeborn American citizens who send a buck across the seas to sell freedom to the poor jerks who live under tyranny.

Your porkchops, your children, your honor, your freedom, your very lives are being rigged every day. You know it. But you don't do anything about it. You're too damned busy worrying about your entertainment. You deserve what you get.

The Curriculum, December 1959

The College matchbook, front & back

IN DEFENSE OF BEATNIKS

EVERYBODY WANTS TO KNOW what a Beatnik is. The term was first used by Herb Caen as a calumny against the Beat Generation of Telegraph Hill, in his column in the *San Francisco Chronicle*. He probably plagiarized it from Al Capp.

David McReynolds, writing in *Liberation* magazine, says "the hipster was here long before *Time* discovered him. And the Beat Generation, by whatever name it is called, is the natural expression of our times, international in character and deeply rooted in the chaos of our times."

What makes a Beatnik? This is what it is commonly supposed to be: 1. They use junk or at least pot, as they call it. 2. Odd clothing. 3. Jazz. 4. Unrhymed poetry. 5. Adroitness at living without honest labor.

All right, some of them work, some don't, some are on junk, some are just slobs from nowhere who can't do anything—just like us back in the days of the old Dil Pickle Club thirty years ago. (In those days a lady told me not to come around her tea-room in my "bohemian" clothes and scare her customers.)

But don't put them down, man. Some of these kids paint, or dance, or write. Some of them are way out in the talent department.

Not so long ago I heard a ham who made himself famous play-acting a character of Mickey Spillane's. He was on a radio show with a bunch of young Beatniks from the College of Complexes. Here was this g-r-e-a-t man patronizing these kids all over the stage. Especially Gnomi Gross and Charlie Smith. These kids are nineteen and seventeen respectively.

Now, if there's one thing that I can't stand it's a ham trying to be a philosopher. I've yet to see one ham that ever stood out in the brains department when it came to constructive, creative thinking. Charlie or Gnomi have more on the ball at their tender ages than this joker will have if he lives to be a hundred.

What makes Beats the way they are? Why, the same things that made us in our day. They are expressing the same revolt against authoritarian discipline, conformity, and regimentation we did. The great difference between us is that we had A World to Win. One old beatnik, namely Jack Conroy, titled one of his novels just that.

We hit the marijuana a time or two, we didn't work any more than we had to, sometimes we rhymed our verse and sometimes we didn't. We discovered Sigmund Freud, John Dewey, Walt Whitman and Fred Nietzsche. We joined labor unions and fought for more money for less work. We got on soapboxes in Bughouse Square and hollered our heads off about Sacco and Vanzetti getting the hot squat. Social security and all the other implements of the alleged Welfare State was a battle we inherited from our ancestors.

But we were dynamic. We had somewhere to go and something to do. One of my kids says, "What's the use of saving money? They're going to take me out and shoot me anyway." These kids would like to save the world, too—but *what* world? And *from* what? And for *whom*? For Frank Costello, the gangster who names the mayor of New York City? For his henchman Carmine DeSapio, who names candidates for President? For Werner von Braun, who is devising new H-bombs to blow this world to hell?

What philosopher will the Beat discover? Should he join a union and fight for good old Jimmy Hoffa? The only big social injustice he knows about is the color question. And he has become color blind. He knows of no better way to solve the color question than to ignore it. His interest in the Welfare State is in how long he can keep getting his rockingchair money from the state unemployment service.

On every hand I hear that Beatniks are on their way out. Yet every day I discover a new batch of them becoming more vocal and more eloquent. Here and now I stake my reputation as a prophet on the prognostication that at least one of the Beatnik poets will live. Most of them that I know are under twenty. They've got more protest in their little fingers than all of the poets of Greenwich Village had in their bodies for the last fifty years.

Take a look at the kids that are writing the new verse. Here are some excerpts:

Life is a glimpse through a dirty window of a moving subway train.

In the 27th minute of the final hour the Reader's Digest, Life Magazine, and the Los Angeles telephone directory played "Capture the Flag."

Henny Penny was high on benny [benzedrine] when the sky fell down.

I know him, this pious liberal.

I am born in an age of khaki-colored swaddling clothes, and lain in a Howitzer manger.

These kids are cynical about everything from the great father-image of Eisenhower to the nursery rhymes of childhood. Their whole expression is one of protest. In fact, it is almost the *only* protest in America today. The only other protest is in the churches. But these kids have a hard time believing—in religion or in anything else.

When my generation were Beatniks we *believed*. We believed in the Revolution, the emancipation of the working class, the gains of science, the gifts of art; some even believed in God. A better world was in the making, and we were a part of it. But these kids have no such faith. These kids can't believe. They have seen the revolution come and go. It gave them all that money can buy—material comforts they don't know what to do with. They go barefoot to show their contempt for it.

They have seen our great democracy represented by a general and his official family of thieves from Wall Street and the Mafia. The Russians send Sputnik around the moon while our science spends billions devising new ways to kill people. Our art and literature are represented by the Book-of-the-Month Club and the covers of the *Saturday Evening Post*. And somehow God got lost on a guided missile to Mars.

We talk about Freedom and ask the kids for a buck to sell it to the world, and then—whether they like it or not—we put them in an army, which is the only institution that maintains the old Roman slave system. We talk about honor and hire call-girls to put over our business deals. We blat about good government

153

and let Wall Street and the Mafia pick our candidates.

In our day we were going to change the system. But these kids can't see that as a way out. They have seen the system changed, but the same kind of bastards are still in control. What are the kids going to do? They can't work, they can't fight, they can't soapbox. All the old answers are futile. So they say, "To hell with it." They withdraw. The whole Beatnik movement is one of withdrawal. "I ain't gonna play in such a game. It's from nowhere. I'm going to get so far out you'll have to do something about me. And don't try to put me down, you bastards."

What is the answer? Give them something to believe in. What or how? I don't know. I don't think it's Zen Buddhism. But, if I am not mistaken, it was in a world like this that Christianity first found its roots. Maybe some Beatnik will come along with a new religion.

The Curriculum, February 1960

Newspaper photo of the Beatnik Convention at the College's New York campus, July 1960 (*l.* to *r.*, Bill Smith and Gnomi Gross of the Chicago delegation, and a New York delegate, Ambrose).

A BEATNIK FOR PRESIDENT

LETTER TO LAWRENCE FERLINGHETTI

COLLEGE OF COMPLEXES
Chicago

Mr Lawrence Ferlinghetti
City Lights Book Shop
San Francisco, California
May 11, 1960

Dear Lawrence,
    Am sending you these posters in the hope you will use your clout to get a North Beach delegation to the convention.
    Hope to get the nomination myself but you probably have a better chance than I on account of you are known throughout the country. There will be no chicanery at the convention if I can help it. And I usually can.
    Who gets the nomination is not of primary importance. The main objective is to lampoon the hell out of the powers that be. I'm sure we can all have a hell of a lot of fun doing it. And we may even change some of the cherished beliefs of the squares. As Mark Twain said, "nothing can stand against the assault of laughter."
    Hoping to hear from you I am

Yours for a Better World,
Slim Brundage, Janitor

P.S. I have two publicity men on the payroll. I pledge their assistance to anyone who wins the nomination.

THANKSGIVING

THERE MUST BE *something* to be thankful for, man! Health, Wealth, Wisdom? Longevity, Education, Progress and Liberty? These are all parts of the same thing, according to the philosophers. But we'll list them anyway:

Health: If dandruff, fallen arches, ulcers, prostatitis, halitosis, T.B. and blindness don't knock me off, I'll live till I get my pension.

Wealth: Payroll taxes ain't paid. Income taxes ain't paid. Withholding taxes ain't paid. Sales taxes ain't paid. Water taxes ain't paid. And the Infernal Revenue Service says I owe somewhere between eighteen cents and two hundred thousand bananas for entertainment taxes for the last nine years. Mike Para, the Complex lawyer, is going down to hold Uncle Infernal's hand while I go to New York and try to hustle up some scratch. If Mike doesn't hold on tight enough, Uncle will put a padlock on the door come Tuesday morning before breakfast. Anybody got fifteen cents they can loan me?

Wisdom: Yes, sir, that's the thing I've always been hip on. How do you think I got myself in the shape I'm in?

Longevity: America's average life span is sixty-six years. I'm fifty-seven. Just been turned down by three life insurance companies as the worst kind of risk. By a miracle and the help of whatever socialized medicine we are blessed with I might make it. But our fate is tied to the half of the world who live no longer than thirty years.

Education: I hired an accountant with a B.A. in economics. He couldn't add up the receipts for thirty days without an adding machine. Where else in the world could that happen? Half of the world can't read and write.

Progress: Every day we are progressing faster and faster toward extinction.

Liberty: The founder of the Snivel Liberties Union says we have lost more liberties in the last ten years than at any time since the Civil War.

Peace: If anybody seriously wanted peace there would be a peace plank in the platform of at least one of the major parties.

Yeah, man, I sure got things to be thankful for! But we'll find something if we have to go back to the insane asylum I was born in.

Or maybe I should go back to the time the cop hit me on my bare fanny with a willow switch on the courthouse ledge in St Louis.

Or when I got flogged on a road gang in the Vacation State for eating out of the same pot with my colored brethren.

Or the handouts I begged in Salt Lake City, because I was too young to hold a man's job.

Or the hundreds of nights I spent in union meetings trying to arouse a social conscience (without any success at all).

Or the millions of words I've beaten out of this typewriter, that no one wants to read.

Okay, let's knock it off. Let's get with it on this prayer of thanks to whatever gods may be.

I'm thankful I live in the most dynamic age the world will ever know. Archimedes, Hipparchus, and Euclid probably had more in the mental department than any of the skull-workers of today. But they didn't have the metal to make a chamber to hold the heat to jet a rocket around the moon. It took the combined dynamics of a million brains working day by day to produce that.

Whether man gets to the moon or not is something that is not going to keep me awake. But the things that made that possible are the things that have been keeping this lunger alive for the last forty years. This dynamic has produced the labor unions that have lowered the working day from twelve hours a day to as low as thirty hours per week. It has produced the radicals, the scientists, the social conscience, and the artists that can make this the most enjoyable of all ages if we can get rid of our ulcers.

I'm thankful for the only revolution in America today. Fourteen million people are on the march for equality, like my ancestors a couple centuries ago. The real heroes in that movement are the kids, white and colored, who are manning the picketlines and the lunchcounter sit-ins.

Let me give thanks that I have been a jailbird, Beatnik, hungry bum and underprivileged kid. Also, that I have worked with my hands most of my life. That's the way most of the world lives.

From the typescript; slightly abridged

OUR CANDIDATES

Kennedy, Nixon, Johnson or Lodge,
Cadillac, Chrysler, Lincoln or Dodge,
They all run on gas,
They get you there fast.
But who wants to go where they're going?

"What's good for General Motors is good for us All,"
says Charlie Wilson who gives Ike his orders
every morning before breakfast.
Sure man, that's the square way to do it.
Spend forty billion a year
for new ways to kill people
while three-fifths of the world goes hungry.
That way G.M. can make a fat profit selling rolling stock
to armies ten thousand miles away.
Then some silly second looey can trigger off a hot war
just so he can make himself general
and become President some day.
And we'll pull the contaminated carcass of your kid
        and mine
out of some stinking foxhole
half way round the world.

Dickie and Jackie, Charlie and Ike,
Just so you dig them, they all sound alike.
Balance the budget, cut down the debt,
Keep up the Cold War, make more bombs yet.
But how they can do it I'm too dumb to get.

Send the marines to Cuba, Guatemala and Iraq.
Put the peasants back in peonage
every time they threaten a Wall Street dollar.
Call all the common people Commies who want to
        eat regular.
But shell out our dollars to every dictator
like Trujillo, Batista or Franco
who want to keep the lower classes

158

from getting too big for their britches.
Holler like hell about free elections in Buca,
But don't mention Mississippi
where they haven't had a free election
in sixty-eight years.

Dickie and Jackie, Charlie and Ike.
Hot war, Cold War, they all sound alike.
One billion humans crying for bread,
Feed them some H-bombs, keep them well-fed.
Feed 'em on Freedom—to hell with the meat.
Give 'em a platform—they won't have to eat.

Rattle that saber, make like we want war.
Send U2's and RB47's
streaking in, over, and around the territory
of our recent ally
to make the world safe for the Four Freedoms.
But man, let the world know that we loyal 100-per-cent
    Americans
will fight to the death to enforce the Monroe Doctrine,
the Eisenhower Doctrine and the Truman Doctrine.
I hope all you squares dig what that means, man!
President Monroe said, "Hands off the Western Hemisphere."
Truman said the same for Europe while good old Ike says,
"Keep your cotton-picking hands off the world."
That way we let the universe know
that your kid and mine is committed to die
any time a foreign plane
comes within hundreds of miles of our shores.

Dickie and Jackie, Charlie and Ike.
Just so you dig them, they all sound alike.
Balance the budget, cut down the debt.
Keep up the Cold War, make more bombs yet.
But how they can do it I'm too dumb to get.

The Curriculum, September 1960

WHY WERE WE IN VIETNAM?

In the councils of government, we must guard against the acquisition of unwarranted influence, whether sought or unsought, by the Military-Industrial Complex. The potential for the disastrous rise of misplaced power exists and will persist.

—Dwight David Eisenhower,
January 17, 1961

EVIDENTLY THE UNITED STATES people care not whether they are ripped off or not. It would be futile to recount the ridiculous robberies from the U.S. people by the banditos in the Military-Industrial Complex. We all know about the $650 toilet seats. We also know that the U.S. people re-elected the president who permitted this to happen, with a landslide.

Way back in 1956 the Industrial Workers of the World staged peace parades in Chicago and New York. They were protesting the Vietnam War, which hadn't really started yet but was being promoted by the Military-Industrial Complex and its Defense Department. This great Democracy of ours was loaning a million bucks a day to the French government to keep its Empire intact. Remember? We had just finished a war to end colonialism. Eleven million of you patriots went out to die for it.

But you were told that "we" must stop the "domino theory" from expanding Communism into Southeast Asia. Of course the Vietnamese were inspired by Moscow to break away from France, just like the American colonies back in the 1700s were inspired by France to break with the British Empire. In the 1950s, however, the U.S. was loaning the government of France a million dollars a day.

On D-Day, General Dwight Eisenhower made this statement: "This landing is part of the concerted United Nations plan for the liberation of Europe, made in conjunction with our great Russian allies." But a few years later these great allies were enemies because they were helping those "dirty gooks."

Here were a people, the Vietnamese, who didn't even have anything the people of the U.S. could use. They were half way around the world from us. But "we" were so paranoid we were afraid that they were going to sail their sampans up the Potomac and bomb the Washington Monument.

As fast as the U.S. army would win some territory, the "gooks" would overrun it, in weeks. Since "we" couldn't win a war this way "we" resorted to the "body count." That meant: Kill as many people as you can.

Never in all history was there such a genocidal war as this. We dumped napalm, poison gases, germs and other murdering substances and devices on these defenseless people. Although news was suppressed as much as possible, the stench got so bad that a million Americans marched on Washington to protest it. Our incumbent president entered a couple of primaries to be re-elected, but he was defeated in two states and withdrew his candidacy.

Promising to stop the war, Richard Nixon won the presidency. He kept it going four more years. But of course the Military-Industrial Complex had nothing to do with *that*.

A book on the market titled *In Banks We Trust* tells how some smart operators made billions of dollars getting the heroin trade going again during the Vietnam War. Maybe the Military-Industrial Complex had nothing to do with that, either, but *somebody* made a few billion.

From the typescript

LEARNING TO COMPLAIN
WITHOUT SUFFERING

I WAS IN THE CLINK in 1919 for being a Wobbly. I was run out of Red Bluff, California for being broke. I wore chains in El Paso and stripes in St Augustine for the same reason. I've been investigated by all the law from the ward-heeler to the FBI for running a forum where free speech is guaranteed to one and all.

Brother, I know what the police state is.

* * *

You should have seen all the garbage-cans I slept in. That's how I got round shoulders.

* * *

I'm an extreme libertarian to the last limits of the endurable. I believe in absolute free speech. I'm against jailing people for their opinions or, for that matter, anything else. I'm opposed to most all religions because they throttle opinion. I don't believe in formal education and I'm delighted I never went to a university—other than my own College of Complexes.

* * *

I'm strongly in favor of common sense, common honesty, and common decency. Naturally, this rules me out of any office of public trust or profit in this society.

* * *

Humor seems to be something politicians are afraid to have.

* * *

I've always been allergic to formal instruction. If you want to find something out, the easiest way is to ask someone who knows. The second easiest way is to look it up in the Newberry Library. The hardest way is to go to school and listen to some ignoramus tell you how to cross the street when you came there to learn about the nebular hypothesis.

* * *

Being president emeritus of the Hobo College and Janitor of the College of Complexes, I can speak as one educator to another.

* * *

Let me make our position plain. As long as there is any free speech in this country, the College of Complexes will open its rostrum to anybody it thinks has something worth listening to.

Very likely the concentration camps are not far away. If so, we will be the first victims of them. Until that time, we will operate as we have been. Free speech is not divisible.

* * *

What did we get out of World War II? The privilege of subsidizing our enemies in the hope that they will protect us from our allies. Eleven million went to fight for the Four Freedoms and came home to find twenty million on subversive lists.

* * *

Remember, the U.S.A. didn't get rid of fascism. We still have it. More than that, we support it: Every day a bite is taken out of your pay envelope to support it throughout the world.

* * *

Maybe Communism is a horrible thing. Some of the things I heard about it are almost as bad as things I've seen in Chicago jails.

* * *

I know what the good old USA is doing. We are teaching the world to hate us. We, with our expanding imperialism. We, with our thirty-five hundred military outposts ready to quell any democratic uprising which might be patterned after our American Revolution. In country after country we have put the landlord back on the peasant's back. With all our guns and all our money all we can do is make the people of the world hate us.

* * *

In the U.S.A. we'd rather spend a dollar to kill somebody than a dime to buy milk for a starving kid.

* * *

You can't stop an ideology with bullets, or buy peace with dollars.

* * *

I hear people say, "Everybody should lift themselves up with their own bootstraps." Sure—but what about the millions who don't have any bootstraps?

* * *

Verily, I say unto you assembled here tonight, if you do not become your brother's keeper you shall suffer for your sins of omission.

* * *

Can people govern themselves without cops, courts and jails? I don't think it's an engineering problem. It's a moral problem. People have got to want to live together in peace and amity.

X-CONVICT
X-COLLEGE PRESIDENT

X-HUSBAND
X-BOOTLEGGER

SLIM X BRUNDAGE
OBREGON 285
GUADALAJARA, MEX.

X-PAINTER
X-BARTENDER

X-JANITOR
X-LOVER

ALMOST X-TINCT

A later version of the Slim X calling card

A HOBO/WOBBLY GLOSSARY

beef: *v.* Complain.

bindle: A bedroll containing all of a hobo's possessions; often a blanket tied with a rope.

bindlestiff: A hobo with a bedroll.

blinds: Canvas between railroad cars. When off, a 'bo can ride in comfort.

'bo: Short for hobo.

boomer: Hobo who never stays long in one place.

bucker: The guy who saws trees into logs.

bug: A fan or fanatic.

bughouse: Lunatic asylum; *adj.,* crazy.

bull: A cop.

bum: A nonmigratory nonworker.

can: Police station or jail.

cokehead: Cocaine addict.

con: Railroad conductor, *i.e.,* boss on a train; in other contexts: confidence man, or convict.

crumb: Louse.

dead horse: A debt to be worked off.

ding: *v.* Beg.

dingbat: Any kind of beggar.

doing time: Working out a sentence in a penitentiary.

fee-grabber: Cop who gets fee for each arrest.

Fellow Worker: term by which Wobblies address each other.

finger: *v.* Accuse or identify someone of a crime.

fix: *v.* Bribe.

flip: *v.* Catch a moving train. *Also* fly.

flop: A bed, or place to sleep; *v.,* sleep.

flophouse: Cheap hotel.

fly: *v.* Catch a moving train. *Also* flip.

fruit tramp: Itinerant fruitpicker.

gandy dancer: Railroad track-repairer.

grifter: Grafter.

ham: Actor.

harvest stiff: A migratory farm-worker.

highclimber: The guy who tops a high tree and readies it for logging.

hobo: A migratory worker.

hobohemia: The section of town where the 'boes congregate.

homeguard: Worker who never leaves town. (Dates from World War I).

hoosegow: Jail.

hot: What you are when the law is looking for you.

jack: Money.

jackroller: City-dwelling robber of 'boes, tramps and drunks.

jam: Trouble.

jungle: Camping place for hoboes, near railroad.

jungle buzzard: A bum who begs only from 'boes, tramps and other bums.

kangaroo court: A jailhouse court improvised by prisoners to resolve disputes among themselves.

knowledge box: Country school-house.

lamster: A guy who beats the law out of town.

main stem: Main street in Skid Road.

mooch: To beg on the street.

moocher: A beggar.

monicker: A nickname.

mucker: A shoveler.

mushfakir: Umbrella repairer.

panhandler: A beggar.

parasite: Capitalist; labor's enemy.

pearldiver: Dishwasher.

pie in the sky: The sky pilot's promise of heaven.

pitch: A salesman's speech; *v.,* sell.

pitchman: Salesman with a clever patter.

plant: *v.* Hide.

pling: *v.* Beg.

plinger: A beggar.

privates: House (as in "to ding the privates," *i.e.,* to beg from house to house rather than at stores or on the stem).

punk: Apprentice; beginner.

rap: An indictment before the law.

rat: *v.* Inform on someone to police.

rattler: Freight train.

roll: *v.* Rob.

roundhouse: Stable for locomotives.

scissorbill: A capitalist without any money; a worker without class-consciousness. He has no money of his own, but sides with the boss against his own fellow workers.

shack: Railroad brakeman, who sometimes also served as guard.

scab: Worker who stays on the job during a strike; strikebreaker.

shark: Mancatcher, *i.e.,* employment agent.

Skid Road: Urban habitat of the floating population.

sky pilot: Preacher.

slave: Worker.

slave market: Employment office.

spieler: Storyteller.

stake: A chunk of money between jobs.

stem: City street.

stewbum: A drunken or alcoholic bum.

stir: Jail.

stiff: Unskilled worker. Originally, a corpse—but the stiffs on Skid Road are only half dead.

tamping: A beating. What a cop gives you if you try to get tough with him.

timberbeast: Migratory logger.

town clown: A small town cop.

tree-faller: A guy who chops down trees.

wage-slave: A worker, *i.e.,* producer of the world's wealth, who surrenders nearly the whole product of his toil to a parasite (the boss), accepting as his or her own compensation only the merest pittance, known as wages.

Wobbly: A member of the Industrial Workers of the World (IWW). *Also* Wob.

workingstiff: A worker (see *stiff*).

yegg: Criminal.

SELECTIONS FROM THE *HIPSICON*

Words and Phrases from Chicago's Beatnikville

Bread: Money.

Bug: *v.* Annoy.

Blast: *v.* Tell off, talk.

Cat: A hip male.

Crazy: Adjective indicating approval.

Caper: Event.

Come off it: *v.* Desist.

Cool: Adjective of approval.

Dig: *v.* Understand.

Drag: Dull activity or person.

Dullsville: An unpleasant place.

Far out: Exciting.

Flake out: *v.* Sleep.

Frantic: Extra exciting.

Fuzz: Cops.

Get hip: *v.* Wise up.

Gig: Job.

Hip: In the know.

Hung up: Frustrated.

In orbit: With it, cool, wise.

Kook: A wild character.

Make the scene: *v.* Arrive, attend.

Outfit: What you need to give yourself a shot in the arm with.

Pad: Apartment, room, bed.

Put down: *v.* Disparage, discourage.

Send: *v.* Stimulate, as in "You send me."

Sound the cat: *v.* Extract information.

Split: *v.* Leave.

Square: Ignorant person; a bourgeois.

Swing: Rapport, appeal.

Tuned in: To have understanding.

Way out: Unusual; far out.

BEARDED 'ANTI-PRESIDENTIAL CANDIDATE'

Chicagoan Heads Beatnik 'Slate'

Picture on Picture Page

NEW YORK ⁽ᴬᴾ⁾—The National, International, and Nowhere Beatnik convention last night nominated a bearded Chicago book store operator as its 1960 "anti-Presidential candidate" in five ballots.

Bill Smith, 36, immediately pledged himself to support ᵇ⁻ Bᵉ᪲ ⁿ᪲rty platᶠ rm

to victory over such opponents as Jim the Greek, a Greenwich village resident who had considerable strength up to the fourth ballot, and "Big Brown" [no other name available] of Detroit.

The convention was held in a smoke-filled rᵐᵐ ᪲ⁿ ᵗʰᵉ

here, got no votes. Neither did Slim Brundage, who merely provided free food and sleeping space [on the floor] in his coffee shop for the three dozen beats attending from a dozen or more states.

The Beat convention began Sunday and had its inception when Beats in coffee houses

Chicago American, July 21, 1960

167

SOURCES

The College of Complexes Archives consist of eleven sizeable cartons of documents, mostly from the period 1951–1964, with some earlier and some later material. The Archives include extensive correspondence regarding the College and/or other activities of the Janitor, as well as business and tax records, legal papers, rent receipts, applications for employment, I.O.U.'s, payroll data, and other paperwork pertaining to the day-to-day operations of the College. Also included are numerous magazine articles and newsclippings about the College and its habitués, with especially good collections on the Miss Beatnik contest of 1959 and the following year's Beatnik Party anti-Presidential campaign, and a considerable quantity of College ephemera (flyers, menus, matchbooks, "Schizo" certificates, calling cards, diplomas, photographs, etc.).

The College Archives also include numerous typescripts and manuscripts by Slim Brundage: articles, essays, memoirs, novels, plays, short stories, poems, lecture notes and other writings, as well as several versions of a hobo cookbook and compilations of hobo and hipster slang. It is from this mass of unpublished writings that most of the texts in this book have been drawn.

The specific sources of the texts in "Free Speech in the Heartland" are as follows:

"All You Need to Know About Slim Brundage" was written in 1945 or '46 at the request of a literary agent, and was intended to stimulate publishers' interest in Brundage's first novel. The text published here includes a few brief insertions from other autobiographical sketches.

"Tramping: A Lost Tradition" reproduces most of the undated (*circa* 1964) typescript of that title, with additions from a draft of Brundage's later hobo song anthology.

The first two paragraphs of "An Old-Time Wobbly Speaks Out" are excerpted from a 1987 lecture on "Free Speech"; the rest is from a late-1940s typescript, "The Red Herring," with a brief concluding passage from *The Curriculum* (August 1956).

"Welcome to Skid Road" is an excerpt from the prologue to the play, "Skid Road" (undated typescript, *circa* late 1930s, early 1940s).

"Chicago's Hobo Colleges" largely reproduces the text of an undated (*circa* 1964) paper of that title, with inserts on Ben Reitman from an earlier text, "The Great Unwashed," and several brief excerpts from Lee Sustar's interviews with Brundage as quoted in his 1983 article in the *Reader* (see Bibliography). The reminiscences of T-Bone Slim are from letters to me dated May 8 and May 29, 1987.

"A Night at the Knowledge Box" is a scene from the play "Skid Road." Several drafts and fragments of drafts of this scene are extant. Although earlier ones are clearly set in The Knowledge Box, later versions refer simply to the Hobo College, and the Director is identified as Jack Macbeth.

"Nina Spies" (originally titled "Old Lady") probably dates from the late 1920s or '30s. The text published here also includes a short paragraph on Haymarket from Brundage's lecture on "Free Speech."

"Statistical Slim" (originally titled "Plain Bum"), is one of several typed profiles under the series title, "Thumb Nail Portraits," dating from the late 1930s or early 1940s. Attached to the packet of "Portraits" is a penciled memo from an *Esquire* magazine editor: "Sorry—sketches are hard to place."

"The Cosmic Kid" is a stray page from an early draft of a perhaps uncompleted play, "Kangaroo Court" (*circa* late 1930s or '40s).

The anecdote herein titled "A Run-In With Ben Reitman" is excerpted from a draft of "Tramping."

"Axel Dragstedt" reproduces most of an article in *The Curriculum* (August 1960), with some material from a draft of "Hobo Colleges."

"Memoirs of a Dil Pickler" largely reproduces a January 1964 paper titled "The Great Unwashed," with substantial inserts from an undated but earlier (*circa* 1961) paper, "The Last Refuge of the Pseudo-Intellectual," as well as excerpts from Lee Sustar's interview with Brundage as quoted in the *Reader* (see Bibliography) and *The Curriculum* (December 1954).

"Endsville" reproduces the bulk of the typescript of that title (1961).

"Let's Save Bughouse Square!" is a slightly abridged version of a rough draft titled "The Stench of Bughouse Square," written in June or July 1959.

"Prolegomena to the Complex History of the College of Complexes" reproduces most of the 1963 typescript, "The College of Complexes," with inserts from a semi-fictionalized record of a visit to the College by "Mularkey McCarthy, reporter for *The Daily Dishup*," and from various issues of *The Curriculum*.

"A Janitor's Guide" includes a large part of "The Last Refuge of the Pseudo-Intellectual," supplemented by excerpts from various autobiographical fragments, *The Curriculum* and other publicity material issued by the College.

The short speeches of greeting and good-bye herein titled "Hail and Farewell" reproduce scripts probably prepared in connection with the early Sixties efforts to put the College of Complexes on TV. The versions published here synthesize several drafts, with brief inserts from College promotional material.

With the exception of "Memoirs of a Dil Pickler," which appeared in a very different and much abridged form in the *Chicago Daily News*, the articles in "Free Speech in the Heartland" are—to the best of our knowledge—published here for the first time.

Most of the texts in the "Ravings" section originally appeared in *The Curriculum* under one of two headings: "Ravings" or "Vicissitudes of the Janitor." The versions published here generally follow the typescripts rather than the often abridged printed texts, and in a few cases incorporate pertinent material from other related articles written at the same time.

To the best of our knowledge, the two extra-curricular texts appear here for the first time. These are: "A Beatnik for President" and "Why Were We in Vietnam?" The latter was part of a 1970s/80s series titled "Who Said That?" The short passages titled "Learning to Complain Without Suffering" are excerpted from various published and unpublished writings.

BIBLIOGRAPHY

Abrams, Irving. *Haymarket Heritage: Memoirs of Irving S. Abrams*, edited by Phyllis Boanes and Dave Roediger, with an introduction by Joseph Jacobs (Chicago: Illinois Labor History Society/Charles H. Kerr Publishing Company, 1989). Chicago anarchism, Free Society Group, IWW, Hobo College.

Adelman, William J. *Haymarket Revisited* (Chicago: Illinois Labor History Society, revised edition, 1986). Focused on Haymarket and its legacy, this detailed tour guide is a useful introduction to the history of Chicago labor radicalism.

Algren, Nelson. *Chicago: City on the Make* (Sausalito: Contact Editions, 1961).

Anderson, Nels. *The Hobo: The Sociology of the Homeless Man* (Chicago: University of Chicago Press, 1923). Hobo College, Radical Bookshop, Ben Reitman, Axel Dragstedt. A list of hobo and IWW reading matter on pp. 187–188 consists almost entirely of books published by Charles H. Kerr.

A Salute to the Janitor. Memorial pamphlet prepared by Burr McCloskey and others in November 1990.

Ashbaugh, Carolyn. *Lucy Parsons, American Revolutionary* (Chicago: Charles H. Kerr Publishing Company, 1976). Chicago anarchism, IWW, Hobo College, Dil Pickle.

Baxandall, Rosalyn Fraad, ed. *Words on Fire: The Life and Writing of Elizabeth Gurley Flynn* (New Brunswick: Rutgers University Press, 1987). IWW, Jack Jones.

Beck, Frank O. *Hobohemia* (Rindge, NH: Richard R. Smith, 1956). Bughouse Square, Martha Biegler, Jack Jones.

Bird, Stewart, with Deborah Shaffer and Dan Georgakas, eds. *Solidarity Forever: An Oral History of the Industrial Workers of the World* (Chicago: Lake View Press, 1985).

Boanes, Phyllis, and Dave Roediger, eds. *See* Abrams, Irving.

Boyd, Neva Leona. *Play and Game Theory in Group Work: A Collection of Papers*, edited and introduced by Paul Simon (Chicago: The Jane Addams Graduate School of Social Work, University of Illinois at Chicago Circle, 1971).

Brennan, Gerald. *"Big Table,"* in *Chicago History*, XVII: 1 & 2 (Chicago, Spring and Summer 1988), 4–23. On the University of Chicago's suppression of a Beat issue of *Chicago Review*, and the travails of its short-lived successor, *Big Table*. For a more detailed account, see the following entry.

—. "Naked Censorship: The True Story of the University of Chicago and William S. Buroughs' *Naked Lunch*," in the *Reader* (Chicago, 29 September 1995, pp. 1, 15–26, and continued in the issue of 6 October, pp. 8–28.

Bronté, Patricia. *Vittles and Vice: An Extraordinary Guide to What's Cooking on Chicago's Near North Side* (Chicago: Henry Regnery, 1952). A restaurant guide and cookbook, with interesting chapters on the Dil Pickle Club, Bughouse Square and Riccardo's.

Brundage, Slim. *Ravings by Manic Depressive* (Chicago and New York: College of Complexes, 1960). A publishing fiasco, this booklet of the Janitor's editorials from *The Curriculum* is full of typographical errors and incorrectly laid out, so that the text is not consecutive.

—-, ed. *The Curriculum: Official Neurosis of the College of Complexes* (Chicago, 1952–61). A calendar of College activities, with commentary by the Janitor (and sometimes others) in almost every issue.

—-, ed. *Hipsicon from the College of Complexes* (Chicago: College of Complexes, 1960). A mimeographed flyer defining seventy-five Beat words and phrases.

Bruns, Roger A. *The Damnedest Radical: The Life and World of Ben Reitman, Chicago's Celebrated Social Reformer, Hobo King, and Whorehouse Physician* (Urbana: University of Illinois Press, 1987). Bughouse Square, Hobo College, Dil Pickle, etc.

Buhle, Mari Jo, with Paul Buhle and Dan Georgakas, eds. *Encyclopedia of the American Left* (New York: Garland, 1990; reissued as a University of Illinois paperback in 1992). Beat Generation, Dada, IWW, Charles H. Kerr Company, Proletarian Party, Surrealism.

Buhle, Paul. "Great Moments in Agitpop: The Kerr Company's Rad-Lit Revival," *Voice Literary Supplement* (New York, September 1985), 24–25.

Bush-Banks, Olivia Ward. *The Collected Works of Olivia Ward Bush-Banks*, compiled and edited by Bernice F. Guillaume (New York: Oxford, 1991). Abraham Lincoln Center Forum, Chicago's Bohemia.

Carlozo, Lou. "William Smith, Voice for Beat Generation," obituary in the *Chicago Tribune*, "Metro Chicago" section, 17 December 1995, 8.

Carnevali, Emanuel. *The Autobiography of Emanuel Carnevali* (New York: Horizon Press, 1967). Dil Pickle, Jack Jones, Radical Bookshop.

Chaplin, Ralph. *Wobbly: The Rough-and-Tumble Story of an American Radical* (Chicago: University of Chicago Press, 1948). IWW, the Charles H. Kerr Company, Dil Pickle, Jack Jones, Radical Bookshop.

The Charles H. Kerr Company Archives, 1885–1985: A Century of Socialist & Labor Publishing (Chicago: Beasley Books in association with the Charles H. Kerr Publishing Company, 1985). A guide to the extensive archives now at Newberry Library.

Cochran, David. "The Charles H. Kerr Company: Books to Change the World," in Sanford Berman and James P. Danky, eds., *Alternative Library Literature, 1990–91: A Biennial Anthology* (Jefferson, NC: McFarland & Co., 1991), 95–99.

Collin, Dorothy. "Can Bughouse Square Revive?" *Chicago Tribune*, 23 June 1980.

Dolgoff, Sam. *Fragments: A Memoir. Personal Recollections Drawn from a Lifetime of Struggle in the Cause of Anarchism* (London: Refract Editions, 1986). Chicago anarchism, Free Society Group, IWW, Ben Reitman.

Drake, St Clair, and Horace R. Cayton. *Black Metropolis: A Study of*

Negro Life in a Northern City (New York: Harper & Row, 1962; first published 1945). Introduction by Richard Wright.

Drury, John. *Chicago in Seven Days* (New York: Robert McBride & Co., 1928; reprinted with appendix, 1930). Radical Bookshop, Studio Players, Bughouse Square, Dil Pickle.

Fagin, Sophia. *Public Forums in Chicago* (M.A. Thesis, Department of Sociology, University of Chicago, 1939). The best survey. Bug Club, Bughouse Square, Hobo College, Radical Bookshop, Dil Pickle, Knowledge Box.

Farrell, James T. *Studs Lonigan: A Trilogy* (New York: Modern Library, 1938). Pages 307–314 feature a visit to the South Side Bug Club, and describes a talk by John Loughman ("John Connolly" in the book).

Flynn, Elizabeth Gurley. *The Rebel Girl: An Autobiography. My First Life (1906–1926)* (New York: International Publishers, revised edition, 1973). IWW, Jack Jones.

—. *See also* Baxandall, ed.

Gazell, James Albert. "The High Noon of Chicago's Bohemias," in the *Journal of the Illinois Historical Society* (Springfield, 1972), 54–68.

Gibson, Morgan. *Revolutionary Rexroth: Poet of East-West Wisdom* (Hamden, Connecticut: Archon Press, 1986).

Goldman, Emma. *Living My Life* (New York: Garden City Publishing Company, 1934). Chicago anarchism, Ben Reitman.

Green, Archie. *Wobblies, Pile Butts, and Other Heroes: Laborlore Explorations* (Urbana: University of Illinois Press, 1993).

—. *Calf's Head & Union Tale: Labor Yarns at Work and Play* (Urbana: University of Illinois Press, 1996).

Haywood, Harry. *Black Bolshevik: Autobiography of an Afro-American Communist* (Chicago: Liberator Press, 1978). Bug Club, Dil Pickle, African Blood Brotherhood.

Haywood, William D. *The Autobiography of Big Bill Haywood* (New York: International Publishers, 1929). IWW, the Charles H. Kerr Company, Radical Bookshop.

Hecht, Ben. *A Child of the Century* (New York: Simon and Schuster, 1954). Dada, Chicago Bohemia.

Heise, Kenan. "Off-Beat Slim Brundage," obituary in the *Chicago Tribune*, reprinted in *A Salute to Slim Brundage, op. cit.*

Jacoby, Russell. *The Last Intellectuals.* (New York: Basic Books, 1987).

Kornbluh, Joyce L., ed. *Rebel Voices: An IWW Anthology* (Chicago: Charles H. Kerr Publishing Company, new and expanded edition, 1988). A good section on the IWW's Free-Speech Fights.

Kreymborg, Alfred. *Troubadour: An Autobiography* (New York: Boni and Liveright, 1925). Dil Pickle.

Leonard, William. "The College of Cut-Ups." *Chicago Tribune Magazine* (May 13, 1956), 27. On the College of Complexes.

———. "In Chicago, We're Mostly Unbeat." *Chicago Tribune Magazine* (November 9, 1958), 8–9. Dil Pickle, College of Complexes.

———. "Chicago's New 'Left Bank.'" *Chicago Tribune Magazine* (November 23, 1958), 27, 30. College of Complexes.

Lipton, Lawrence. *The Holy Barbarians* (New York: Julian Messner, 1959). The first study of the Beats, with mentions of the Chicago scene and long quotations from Joffre Stewart, 301–304.

Lynd, Alice and Staughton, eds. *Rank and File: Personal Histories by Working-Class Organizers* (Boston: Beacon Press, 1974). Interview with Burr McCloskey, 149–162.

Maass, Alan. "The Little Red Book House," *Reader* (Chicago, 17 October 1986), 1, 12–32. Charles H. Kerr Company, IWW, Fred Thompson.

McCloskey, Burr. "The High Price of Free Speech." A letter in the *Reader* (Chicago, December 9, 1983).

———. *See also* Lynd, above.

McDarrah, Fred W. *Kerouac and Friends: A Beat Generation Album* (New York: Morrow, 1985). Photo of Bill Smith at Beatnik Party convention, 171.

McGuckin, Henry E. *Memoirs of a Wobbly* (Chicago: Charles H. Kerr Publishing Company, 1987). An IWW *On the Road*; one of the best accounts of pre-World-War-I hoboing.

McWhinnie, Chuck. "Myron Brundage. ex-owner of College of Complexes pubs," in the *Chicago Sun-Times*, 1 November 1990.

Murray, George. "There's Free Speech Aplenty." *Chicago American* (25 March 1959). Bughouse Square, Dil Pickle, Cosmic Kid, Dave Tullman, John Loughman, College of Complexes.

Niver, Joseph, ed. *Earth: A History* (Millwood, New York: KTQ Press, 1977). Facsimile reprint, with detailed introduction, appendices and index, of an important Chicago "little mag" of the 1930s; contributors include Dil Picklers James T. Farrell, Ralph Chaplin and Jack Jones himself. Several issues were printed by Jones's Dil Pickle Press.

"Nobody Here But Us Presidential Candidates." *Newsweek* (August 22, 1960) 21–22. A survey of Third-Party Presidential candidates, including the Beatnik Party's anti-candidate, Bill Smith.

Park, Robert E., with Ernest W. Burgess. *The City* (Chicago: University of Chicago Press, 1967; first published 1925).

Parry, Albert. *Garrets and Pretenders: A History of Bohemianism in America* New York: Dover, 1960; originally published by Covici-Friede in 1933). Includes reminiscences of the Dil Pickle by Edna Fine Dexter, 201–208.

Powers, Joe, and Mark Rogovin. *The Day Will Come: Stories of the Haymarket Martyrs and the Men and Women Buried Alongside the Monument* (Chicago: Published for the Illinois Labor History Society by the Charles H. Kerr Company, 1994). Includes biographical sketches of August Spies, Nina Spies, Ben Reitman, Fred Thompson, Slim Brundage and many others.

Putnam, Samuel. *Paris Was Our Mistress: Memoirs of a Lost and Found*

Generation (Carbondale: Southern Illinois University Press, 1970; originally published by Viking Press, 1947). Dil Pickle.

Reitman, Ben. *Life Among the Outcasts.* Typescript of unpublished autobiography, in the Charles H. Kerr Publishing Company Archives at Newberry Library, Chicago.

—."Life and Death of the Dill [sic] Pickle," the *Chicago Sunday Times*, 2 August 1937, 20–21.

—, ed. *Sister of the Road: The Autobiography of Box-Car Bertha* (New York: Macaulay, 1937). Bughouse Square, Dil Pickle, Lucy Parsons, Nina Spies, Martha Biegler.

Rexroth, Kenneth. *An Autobiographical Novel* (Weybridge, Surrey, U.K.: Whittet Books, 1977). Bug Club, Bughouse Square, the Charles H. Kerr Company, African Blood Brotherhood, Dada, Radical Bookshop, Studio Players, Dil Pickle, Jack Jones.

Roediger, Dave. "100 Years Young: The Charles H. Kerr Company," in *Canadian Dimension* (Fall, 1986), 16–18.

—, ed. *See* Thompson, Fred.

—, and Franklin Rosemont, eds. *Haymarket Scrapbook* (Chicago: Charles H. Kerr Publishing Company, 1986). Chicago anarchism, IWW, Charles H. Kerr Company; sketches of and/or texts by Lucy Parsons, Nina Spies, Fred Thompson, Sam Dolgoff, Emma Goldman and many more.

Rosemont, Franklin. "Dada," in Buhle et al., *Encyclopedia of the American Left, op. cit.*

—. "Joe Giganti and the Reviving of the Charles H. Kerr Publishing Company," in *The Match!* (Tucson, Arizona, Fall-Winter 1986–87), 22–25.

—. "Proletarian Party," in Buhle *et al., Encyclopedia of the American Left, op. cit.*

—. "A Short Treatise on Wobbly Cartoons," in Kornbluh, *Rebel Voices: An IWW Anthology, op. cit.*

—, ed. *Juice Is Stranger Than Friction: Selected Writings of T-Bone Slim* (Chicago: Charles H. Kerr Publishing Company, 1992).

—, with Penelope Rosemont and Paul Garon, eds. *The Forecast Is Hot! Tracts and Other Collective Declarations of the Surrealist Movement in the United States, 1966–1976* (Chicago: Black Swan Press, 1997).

Ruff, Allen. "Socialist Publishing in Illinois: Charles H. Kerr & Company," in *Illinois Historical Journal* (Springfield, Vol. 79, Spring 1986), 19–32.

—. *"We Called Each Other Comrade": Charles H. Kerr & Company, Radical Publishers* (Urbana: University of Illinois Press, 1997).

Salerno, Salvatore. *Red November, Black November: Culture and Community in the Industrial Workers of the World* (Albany: State University of New York Press, 1989).

Sawyers, June Skinner. *Chicago Portraits: Biographies of 250 Famous Chicagoans* (Chicago: Loyola University Press, 1991). Jack Conroy, James T. Farrell, Big Bill Haywood, Charles H. Kerr, Mary Marcy, Albert and

Lucy Parsons, Ben Reitman.

—. *Chicago Sketches: Urban Tales, Stories and Legends from Chicago History* (Chicago: Wild Onion, 1995). Slim Brundage, Jack Jones, Ben Reitman, Bughouse Square, Dil Pickle, Radical Bookshop.

Sheridan, Jack. "Where There Ain't No God." Typescript of unpublished reminiscences of Bughouse Square, in the Charles H. Kerr Publishing Company Archives at Newberry Library, Chicago.

Smith, Alson, J. *Chicago's Left Bank* (Chicago: Henry Regnery Company, 1953).

Starrett, Vincent. *Born in a Bookshop: Chapters from the Chicago Renascence* (Norman: University of Oklahoma Press, 1965). Dil Pickle.

Sustar, Lee. "When Speech Was Free (And Usually Worth It). Con Men and Communists, Lowlife and Literati, Blowhards and Bohemians: Reminiscences of Chicago's Soapbox Society." *Reader* (Chicago, October 21, 1983). Mostly on Slim Brundage and the College, with backward glances at the Bug Club, Bughouse Square and the Dil Pickle.

Targ, William. *Indecent Pleasures: The Life and Colorful Times of William Targ* (New York: Macmillan, 1975).

—-, and Lewis Herman. *The Case of Mr. Cassidy* (New York: Phoenix Press, 1939). Mystery novel set in the Near North Side. Bughouse Square, Dave Tullman.

Terkel, Studs. *Chicago* (New York: Pantheon, 1986).

Thompson, Bertha. See Reitman, ed.

Thompson, Fred. *Fellow Worker: The Life of Fred Thompson*, edited and introduced by Dave Roediger (Chicago: Charles H. Kerr Publishing Company, 1993). IWW, T-Bone Slim, Proletarian Party, the Charles H. Kerr Company.

—-. *The IWW: Its First Seventy Years*, with an update by Patrick Murfin (Chicago: Industrial Workers of the World, 1976).

Tuthill, Jack. *Sideshow of a Big City: Tales of Yesterday and Today* (Chicago: Kenfield-Leach, 1932). Maxwell Street (35–40), Radical Bookshop and Studio Players (212–222).

Weil, "Yellow Kid." *"Yellow Kid" Weil: The Autobiography of America's Master Swindler* (Chicago: Ziff-Davis, 1948). Dil Pickle, Jack Jones.

Wentworth, Edward Chichester. *After the Eleventh Hour* (Chicago: Wilmerding Press, 1928). A curious novel set on the Near North Side. Bughouse Square, Dil Pickle, Radical Bookshop, Studio Players.

Wixson, Douglas. *Worker-Writer in America: Jack Conroy and the Tradition of Midwestern Literary Radicalism, 1898–1990* (Urbana: University of Illinois Press, 1994).

Yelensky, Boris. "Twenty-Five Years of 'Free Society' Activity in Chicago," in *The World Scene From the Libertarian Point of View* (Chicago: Free Society Group, 1951), 90–94.

Zorbaugh, Harvey W. *The Gold Coast and the Slum* (Chicago: University of Chicago Press, 1929). Bughouse Square, Dil Pickle.

BOOKS *for a* BETTER WORLD